I0670977

RUTH FIELDING ON CLIFF ISLAND

OR, THE OLD HUNTER'S TREASURE BOX

ALICE B. EMERSON

1st WORLD
LIBRARY
Literary Society

Ruth Fielding on Cliff Island

Alice B. Emerson

© 1st World Library, 2007
PO Box 2211
Fairfield, IA 52556
www.1stworldlibrary.com
First Edition

LCCN: 2007934075

Softcover ISBN: 978-1-4218-9610-6
Hardcover ISBN: 978-1-4218-9710-3
eBook ISBN: 978-1-4218-9510-9

Purchase *"Ruth Fielding on Cliff Island"*
as a traditional bound book at:
www.1stWorldLibrary.com/purchase.asp?ISBN=978-1-4218-9610-6

1st World Library is a literary, educational organization
dedicated to:

- Creating a free internet library of downloadable ebooks

- Hosting writing competitions and offering book publishing
scholarships.

Interested in more 1st World Library books? contact:
literacy@1stworldlibrary.com
Check us out at: www.1stworldlibrary.com

1ˢᵗ World Library Literary Society

Giving Back to the World

"If you want to work on the core problem, it's early school literacy."

- James Barksdale, former CEO of Netscape

"No skill is more crucial to the future of a child, or to a democratic and prosperous society, than literacy."

- Los Angeles Times

"Literacy... means far more than learning how to read and write... The aim is to transmit... knowledge and promote social participation."

- UNESCO

"Literacy is not a luxury, it is a right and a responsibility. If our world is to meet the challenges of the twenty-first century we must harness the energy and creativity of all our citizens."

- President Bill Clinton

"Parents should be encouraged to read to their children, and teachers should be equipped with all available techniques for teaching literacy, so the varying needs and capacities of individual kids can be taken into account."

- Hugh Mackay

CONTENTS

CHAPTER I

THE WRECK AT APPLEGATE CROSSING

A September morning has dawned, with only a vague tang of autumn in the air. In the green old dooryard at the Red Mill, under the spreading shade trees, two girls are shelling a great basket of dried lima beans for the winter's store.

The smaller, black-haired girl begins the conversation.

"Suppose Jane Ann doesn't come, Ruth?"

"You mean on this morning train?" responded the plumper and more mature-looking girl, whose frank face was particularly attractive.

"Yes."

"Then Tom said he would go back to meet the evening train—and we'll go with him," said Ruth Fielding, with a smile. "But I could not go this morning and leave poor Aunt Alvirah all these beans to shell."

"Of course not," agreed her friend, promptly. "And Jane Ann won't feel offended by our not meeting her at Cheslow, I know."

"No, indeed, Helen," laughed Ruth. "Jane Ann Hicks is altogether too sensible a girl."

"Sensible about everything but her name," commented Helen Cameron, making a little face.

"And one can scarcely blame her. It *is* ugly," Ruth responded, with a sigh. "Jane Ann Hicks! Dear, dear! how could her Uncle Bill be so thoughtless as to name her that, when she was left, helpless, to his care?"

"He didn't realize that fashions in names change—like everything else," observed Helen, briskly.

"I wonder what the girls at Briarwood will say to that name," Ruth pondered.

"Why The Fox and Heavy will help us make the other girls toe the mark. And Madge Steele! She's a regiment in herself," declared Helen. "We all had such a fine time at Silver Ranch that the least we can do is to see that Jane Ann is not hazed like the other infants."

"I expect we all have to stand our share of hazing when we go into fresh company," said Ruth, reflectively. "But there will not be the same crowd to meet her that met us, dear."

"And the Sweetbriars will be on hand to preserve order," laughed her chum. "Thanks to *you*, Ruthie. Why—oh! see Tom!"

She jumped up, dropping a lapful of pods, and pointed up the Cheslow road, which here branched from the river road almost opposite the Red Mill.

"What is the matter?" demanded Ruth, also scrambling to

Alice B. Emerson

her feet.

A big touring car was approaching at top speed. They could see that the only person in it was a black-haired boy, who sat at the steering wheel.

He brought the machine to an abrupt stop before the gate, and leaped out. Tearing off his goggles as he ran, he approached the two girls in such a state of excitement that he could scarce speak coherently.

"Oh, Tom! what is it?" gasped Helen, seizing his arm with both hands.

It took but a single glance to discover the relationship between them. Twins never looked more alike—only Tom's features lacked the delicacy of outline which belonged to his sister.

"Tom!" cried Ruth, on the other side of the excited youth, "don't keep us on tenter-hooks. Surely nothing has happened to Jane Ann?"

"I don't know! They won't tell us much about it at the station," exclaimed the boy.

"There hasn't been a wreck?" demanded Ruth.

"Yes. At Applegate Crossing. And it is the train from the west that is in trouble with a freight. A rear-end collision, I understand."

"Suppose something has happened to the poor girl!" wailed Helen.

"We must go and see," declared Ruth, quick to decide in an

emergency. "You must drive us, Tom."

"That's what I came back for," replied Tom Cameron, mopping his brow. "I couldn't get anything out of Mercy's father—"

"Of course not," Helen said, briskly, as Ruth ran to the house. "The railroad employes are forbidden to talk when there is an accident. Mr. Curtis might lose his job as station agent at Cheslow if he answered all queries."

Ruth came flying back from the house. She had merely called into the kitchen to Aunt Alvirah that they were off— and their destination. While Tom sprang in and manipulated the self-starter, his sister and the girl of the Red Mill took their seats in the tonneau.

By the time old Aunt Alvirah had hobbled to the porch, the automobile was being turned, and backed, and then it was off, up the river road. Uncle Jabez, in his dusty garments, appeared for a moment at the door of the mill as they flashed past in the big motor car. Evidently he was amazed to see the three—the girls hatless—starting off at such a pace in the Camerons' car.

Tom threw in the clutch at high speed and the car bounded over the road, gradually increasing its pace until the hum of the engine almost drowned out all speech. The girls asked no questions. They knew that, by following the river road along the placid Lumano for some distance, they could take a fork toward the railway and reach Applegate Crossing much quicker than by going through Cheslow.

Once Tom flung back a word or two over his shoulder. No relief train had gone from their home station to the scene of the wreck. It was understood that a wrecking gang, and doctors, and nurses, had started from the distant city before ever the Cheslow people learned of the trouble.

"Oh! if Jane Ann should be hurt!" murmured Helen for the twentieth time.

"Uncle Bill Hicks would be heartbroken," agreed Ruth.

Although the crossroad, when they struck into it at the Forks, was not so smooth and well-built as the river highway, Tom did not reduce speed. Mile after mile rolled away behind them. From a low ridge they caught a glimpse of the cut where the two trains had come together.

It was the old story of a freight being dilatory in getting out of a block that had been opened for the passage of an express. The express had run her nose into the caboose of the freight, and more harm was done to the freight than to the passenger cars. A great crowd, however, had gathered about.

Tom ran the car into an open lot beside the tracks, where part of the railroad fence had been torn away. Two passenger cars were on their sides, and one or two of the box cars had burst open.

"Look at that!" gasped the boy, whose bright eyes took in much that the girls missed, for *they* were looking for Jane Ann Hicks. "That's a menagerie car—and it's all smashed. See! 'Rival's Circus & Menagerie.' Crickey! suppose some of the savage animals are loose!"

"Oh! don't suggest such a thing," begged his sister.

Tom saw an excited crowd of men near the broken cage cars of the traveling menagerie. Down in the gully that was here crossed by the narrow span of the railroad trestle, there was a thick jungle of saplings and brush out of which a few taller trees rose, their spreading limbs almost touching the sides of the ravine.

It must be confessed that the boy was drawn more toward this point of interest than toward the passenger train where Jane Ann might possibly be lying injured. But Ruth and Helen ran toward this latter spot, where the crowd of passengers was thickest.

Suddenly the crowd parted and the girls saw a figure lying on the ground, with a girl about their own age bending over it. Ruth screamed, "Jinny!" and at the sound of the pet name her uncle's cow punchers had given her, the girl from Silver Ranch responded with an echoing cry.

"Oh, Ruth! And Helen! I'm not hurt—only scratched. But this poor fellow—"

"Who is he?" demanded Helen Cameron, as she and Ruth arrived beside their friend.

The figure on the ground was a very young man—a boy, in fact. He was roughly dressed, and sturdily built. His eyes were closed and he was very pale.

"He got me out of the window when the car turned over," gasped Jane Ann. "Then he fell with me and has either broken his leg, or twisted it—"

"Only strained, Miss," spoke the victim of the accident, opening his eyes suddenly. Ruth saw that they were kind, brown eyes, with a deal of patience in their glance. He was not the sort of chap to make much of a trifle.

"But you can't walk on it," exclaimed Jane Ann, who was a large-framed girl with even blacker hair than Helen's—

Alice B. Emerson

straight as an Indian's—and with flashing eyes. She was expensively dressed, although her torn frock and coat were not in very good taste. She showed plainly a lack of that motherly oversight all girls need.

"They'll come and fix me up after a time," said the strange youth, patiently.

"That won't do," declared Ruth, quickly. "I suppose the doctors are busy up there with other passengers?"

"Oh, yes," admitted Jane Ann. "Lots of people were hurt in the cars a good deal worse than Mr.—Mr.—?"

"My name's Jerry Sheming, Miss," said the youth. "Don't you worry about me."

"Here's Tom!" cried Helen. "Can't we lift him into the car? We'll run to Cheslow and let Dr. Davison look at his leg," she added.

Tom, understanding the difficulty at a glance, agreed. Between the four young folk they managed to carry Jerry Sheming to the car. They had scarcely got him into the tonneau when a series of yells arose from the crowd down near the derailed freight train.

"Look out! Take care of that panther! I told you she was out!" shouted one voice above the general uproar.

Ruth Fielding and her friends, startled indeed, ran to the brow of the hill. One of the wide-branched trees rose from the bottom of the ravine right below them. Along one of the branches lay a long, cat-like body.

"A black panther!" gasped Tom.

CHAPTER II

THE PANTHER AT LARGE

"Say! let's get out of here!" exclaimed the girl from the West. "I don't want to be eaten up by that cat—and Uncle Bill would make an awful row over it. Come on!"

She seized Ruth's hand and, leaving Tom to drag his sister with him, set off at full speed for the motor car, wherein Jerry Sheming, the stranger, still lay helpless.

Helen was breathless from laughter when she reached the car. Jane Ann's desire not to be eaten up by the panther because of what Mr. Bill Hicks, of Bullhide, Montana, would say, was so amusing that Tom's twin forgot her fright.

"Stop your fooling and get in there—quick!" commanded the anxious boy, pushing his sister into the tonneau. With the injured Jerry, the back of the car was well filled. Tom leaped into the front seat and tried to start the car.

"Quick, Tom!" begged Ruth Fielding. "There's the panther."

"Panther! What panther?" demanded Jerry, starting up in his seat.

Alice B. Emerson

The lithe, black beast appeared just then over the brow of the hill. The men who had started after the beast were below in the ravine, yelling, and driving the creature toward them. The motor car was the nearest object to attract the great cat's wrath, and there is no wild beast more savage and treacherous.

Tom was having trouble in starting the car. Besides, it was headed directly for the huge cat, and the latter undoubtedly had fastened its cruel gaze upon the big car and its frightened occupants.

Ruth Fielding and her friends had been in serious difficulties before. They had even (in the woods of the Northern Adirondacks and in the foothills of the Montana Rockies) met peril in a somewhat similar form. But here, with the panther creeping toward them, foot by foot, the young friends had no weapon of defense.

Ruth had often proved herself both a courageous and a sensible girl. Coming from her old home where her parents had died, a year and a half before, she had received shelter at the Red Mill, belonging to her great uncle, Jabez Potter, at first as an object of charity, for Uncle Jabez was a miserly and ill-tempered old fellow. The adventures of the first book of this series, entitled "Ruth Fielding of the Red Mill; Or, Jasper Parloe's Secret," narrate how Ruth won her way—in a measure, at least—to her uncle's heart.

Ruth made friends quickly with Helen and Tom Cameron, and when, the year previous, Helen had gone to Briarwood Hall to school, Ruth had gone with her, and the fun, friendships, rivalries, and adventures of their first term at boarding school are related in "Ruth Fielding at Briarwood Hall; Or, Solving the Campus Mystery."

In "Ruth Fielding at Snow Camp; Or, Lost in the Back-woods," the third volume of the series, are told the mid-winter sports of our heroine and her friends; and later, after the school year is concluded, we find them all at the seaside home of one of the Briarwood girls, and follow them through the excitement and incidents of "Ruth Fielding at Lighthouse Point; Or, Nita, the Girl Castaway."

When our present story opens Ruth and the Camerons have just returned from the West, where they had spent a part of the summer vacation with Jane Ann Hicks, and their many adventures are fully related in the fifth volume of the series, entitled "Ruth Fielding at Silver Ranch; Or, Schoolgirls Among the Cowboys."

Few perils they had faced, however, equalled this present incident. The black panther, its gleaming eyes fixed upon the stalled motor car and the young folk in it, crouched for only a moment, with lashing tail and bared fangs.

Uttering another half-stifled snarl, the beast bounded into the air. The distance was too great for the brute to pass immediately to the car; but it was plain that one more leap would bring her aboard.

"Start it! Quick, Tom!" gasped Helen.

"I—I can't!" groaned her brother.

"Then we must run—"

"Sit still!" commanded Jane Ann, with fire in her eye. "I'm not going to run from that cat. I hate 'em, anyway—"

"We can't leave Mr. Sheming," said Ruth, decidedly. "Try again, Tommy."

Alice B. Emerson

"Oh, don't bother about me," groaned the young man, who was still a stranger to them. "Don't be caught here on my account."

"It will not do us any good to run," cried Ruth, sensibly. "Oh, Tommy!"

And then the engine started. The electric starter had worked at last. Tom threw in his clutch and the car lunged ahead just as the snarling cat sprang into the air again.

The cat and the car were approaching each other, head on. The creature could not change its course; nor could Tom Cameron veer the car very well on this rough ground.

He had meant to turn the car in a big circle and make for the road again. But that flashing black body darting through the air was enough to shake the nerve of anybody. The car "wabbled." It shot towards the tracks, and then back again.

Perhaps that was a happy circumstance, after all. For as the car swerved, there was a splintering crash, and the windshield was shivered. The body of the panther shot to one side and the motor car escaped the full shock of the charge.

Over and over upon the ground the panther rolled; and off toward the road, in a long, sweeping curve, darted the automobile.

"Lucky escape!" Tom shouted, turning his blazing face once to look back at the party in his car.

"Oh! More than luck, Tommy!" returned Ruth, earnestly.

"It was providential," declared Helen, shrinking into her seat again and beginning to tremble, now that the danger was past.

"Good hunting!" exclaimed the girl from the ranch. "Think of charging a wildcat with one of these smoke wagons! My! wouldn't it make Bashful Ike's eyes bulge out? I reckon he wouldn't believe we had such hunting here in the East—eh?" and her laugh broke the spell of fear that had clutched them all.

"That critter beats the biggest bobcat I ever heard of," remarked Jerry Sheming. "Why! a catamount isn't in it with that black beast."

"Where'd it go?" asked Tom, quite taken up with the running of the car.

"Back to the ravine," said Ruth. "Oh! I hope it will do no damage before it is caught."

Just now the four young friends had something more immediate to think about. This Jerry Sheming had been "playing 'possum." Suddenly they found that he lay back in the tonneau, quite insensible.

"Oh, oh!" gasped Helen. "What shall we do? He is—Oh, Ruth! he isn't *dead*?"

"Of a strained leg?" demanded Jane Ann, in some disgust.

"But he looks so white," said Helen, plaintively.

"He's just knocked out. It's hurt him lots more than he let on," declared the girl from Silver Ranch, who had seen many a man suffer in silence until he lost the grip on himself—as this youth had.

Alice B. Emerson

In half an hour the car stopped before Dr. Davison's gate—the gate with the green lamps. Jerry Sheming had come to his senses long since and seemed more troubled by the fact that he had fainted than by the injury to his leg.

Ruth, by a few searching questions, had learned something of his story, too. He had not been a passenger on the train in which Jane Ann was riding when the wreck occurred. Indeed, he hadn't owned carfare between stations, as he expressed it.

"I was hoofin' it from Cheslow to Grading. I heard of a job up at Grading—and I needed that job," Jerry had observed, drily.

This was enough to tell Ruth Fielding what was needed. When Dr. Davison asked where the young fellow belonged, Ruth broke in with:

"He's going to the mill with me. You come after us, Doctor, if you think he ought to go to bed before his leg is treated."

"What do you reckon your folks will say, Miss?" groaned the injured youth. And even Helen and Tom looked surprised.

"Aunt Alvirah will nurse you," laughed Ruth. "As for Uncle Jabez—"

"It will do Uncle Jabez good," put in Dr. Davison, confidently. "That's right, Ruthie. You take him along to your house. I'll come right out behind you and will be there almost before Tom, here, and your uncle's Ben can get our patient to bed."

It had already been arranged that Jane Ann should go on to Outlook, the Camerons' home. She would remain there with the twins for the few days intervening before the young folk went back to school—the girls to Briarwood, and Tom to Seven Oaks, the military academy he had entered when his sister and Ruth went to their boarding school.

"How you will ever get your baggage—and in what shape—we can only guess," Tom said to the Western girl, grinning over his shoulder as the car flew on toward the Red Mill. "Guess you'll have to bid a fond farewell to all the glad rags you brought with you, and put on some of Ruth's, or Helen's."

"I'd look nice; wouldn't I?" she scoffed, tossing her head. "If I don't get my trunks I'll sue the railroad company."

The car arrived before the gate of the cottage. There was the basket of beans just where Ruth and Helen had left them. And Aunt Alvirah came hobbling to the door again, murmuring, "Oh, my back! and oh, my bones!" and quite amazed when she saw Ben come running to help Tom Cameron into the house with the youth from the railroad wreck.

"Though, landy's sake! I don't know what your Uncle Jabez will say when he comes back from town and finds this boy in the best bed," grumbled Aunt Alvirah, after a bit, when she and Ruth were left alone with Jerry Sheming, and the others had gone on in the car, hurrying so as not to be late for luncheon at Outlook.

Alice B. Emerson

CHAPTER III

UNCLE JABEZ HAS TWO OPINIONS

Dr. Davison came, found that Jerry's leg was not broken, left liniment, some quieting medicine to use if the patient could not sleep, and went away. Still Uncle Jabez had not returned from town.

Dinner had been a farce. Ben, the hired man, was fed as usual; but Ruth and Aunt Alvirah did not feel like eating; and, considering his fever, it was just as well, the doctor said, if the patient did not eat until later.

Jerry Sheming was a fellow of infinite pluck. The pain he had endured during his rough ride in the automobile must have been terrific. Yet he was only ashamed, now, that he had fainted.

"First time I ever heard of a Sheming fainting—or yet a Tilton, Miss," he told Ruth.

"I don't believe you belong near here?" suggested Ruth, who sat beside him, for he seemed restless. "I don't remember hearing either of those names around the Red Mill."

"No. I—I lived away west of here," replied Jerry, slowly.

"Oh, a long ways."

"Not as far as Montana? That is where Jane Ann comes from."

"The girl I helped through the car window?" he asked, quickly.

"Yes. Miss Hicks."

"I did not mean really West," he said. "But it's quite some miles. I had been walking two days—and I'm some walker," he added, with a smile.

"Looking for work, you said?" questioned Ruth, diffident about showing her interest in the young fellow, yet deeply curious.

"Yes. I've got to support myself some way."

"Haven't you any folks at all, Mr. Jerry?"

"I ain't a 'mister,'" said the youth. "I'm not so much older than you and your friends."

"You seem a lot older," laughed Ruth, tossing back her hair.

"That's because I have been working most of my life—and I guess livin' in the woods all the time makes a chap seem old."

"And you've lived in the woods?"

"With my uncle. I can't remember anybody else belongin' to me—not very well. Pete Tilton is *his* name. He's been a guide and hunter all his life. And of late years he got so

Alice B. Emerson

queer—before they took him away—"

"Took him away?" interrupted Ruth, "What do you mean by that?"

"Why, I'll tell you," said Jerry, slowly. "He got wild towards the last. It was something about his money and papers that he lost. He kep' 'em in a box somewhere. There was a landslide at the west end of the island."

"The island? What island?"

"Cliff Island. That's where we lived. Uncle Pete said he owned half the island, but Rufe Blent cheated him out of it. That's what made him so savage with Blent, and he come pretty near killin' him. At least, Blent told it that way.

"So they took poor Uncle Pete into court, and they said he wasn't safe to be at large, and sent him to the county asylum. Then—well, there wasn't no manner o' use my stayin' around there. Rufe Blent warned me off the island. So I started out to hunt a job."

The details were rather vague, but Ruth felt a little diffident about asking for further particulars. Besides, it was not long before Uncle Jabez came home.

"What do ye reckon your Aunt Alvirah keeps that spare room for?" demanded the old miller, with his usual growl, when Ruth explained about Jerry. "For to put up tramps?"

"Oh, Uncle! he isn't just a *tramp*!"

"I'd like to know what ye call it, Niece Ruth?" grumbled Uncle Jabez.

"Think how he saved Jane Ann! That car was rolling right down the embankment. He pulled her through the window and almost the next moment the car slid the rest of the way to the bottom, and lots of people—people in the chairs next to her—were badly hurt. Oh, Uncle! he saved her life, perhaps."

"That ain't makin' it any dif'rent," declared Uncle Jabez. "He's a tramp and nobody knows anything about him. Why didn't Davison send him to the hospital? The doc's allus mixin' us up with waifs an' strays. He's got more cheek than a houn' pup—"

"Now, Jabez!" cried the little old lady, who had been bending over the stove. "Don't ye make yourself out wuss nor you be. That poor boy ain't doin' no harm to the bed."

"Makin' you more work, Alviry."

"What am I good for if it ain't to work?" she demanded, quite fiercely. "When I can't work I want ye sh'd take me back to the poor farm where ye got me—an' where I'd been these last 'leven years if it hadn't been for your charity that you're so 'fraid folks will suspect—"

"Charity!" broke in Uncle Jabez. "Ha! Yes! a fat lot of charity I've showed you, Alviry Boggs. I reckon I've got my money's wuth out o' you back an' bones."

The old woman stood as straight as she could and looked at the grim miller with shining eyes. Ruth thought her face really beautiful as she smiled and said, wagging her head at the gray-faced man:

"Oh, Jabez Potter! Jabez Potter! Nobody'll know till you're in your coffin jest how much good you've done in this world'—

Alice B. Emerson

on the sly! An' you'll let this pore boy rest an' git well here before he has to go out an' hunt a job for hisself. For my pretty, here, tells me he ain't got no home nor no friends."

"Uh-huh!" grunted Uncle Jabez, and stumped away to the mill, fairly beaten for the time.

"He grumbles and grunts," observed Aunt Alvirah, shaking her head as she turned to her work again. "But out o' sight he's re'lly gettin' tender-hearted, Ruthie. An' I b'lieve you showed him how a lot. Oh, my back! and oh, my bones!"

Before supper time a man on horseback came to the mill and cried a warning to the miller and his family: "Look out for your stables and pigpens. There's three beasts loose from those wrecked menagerie cars at the crossing, Jabez."

"Mercy on us! They ain't bound this way, are they?" demanded Uncle Jabez, with more anxiety than he usually showed.

"Nobody knows. You know, the piece of woods yonder is thick. The menagerie men lost them an hour ago. A big black panther—an ugly brute—and a lion and lioness. Them last two they say is as tame as kittens. But excuse me! I'd ruther trust the kittens," said the neighbor. Then he dug his heels in the sides of his horse and started off to bear the news to other residents along the road that followed this bank of the Lumano River.

Jabez shouted for Ben to hurry through his supper, and they closed the mill tight while the womenfolk tried to close all the shutters on the first floor of the cottage. But the "blinds" had not been closed on the east side of the house since they were painted the previous spring. Aunt Alviry was the kind of housekeeper who favored the morning sun and it always streamed into the windows of the guest room.

When they tried to close the outside shutters of those windows, one had a broken hinge that the painters had said nothing about. The heavy blind fell to the ground.

"Goodness me!" exclaimed Ruth, running back into the house. "That old panther could jump right into that room where Jerry is. But if we keep a bright light in there all night, I guess he won't—if he comes this way at all."

It was foolish, of course, to fear the coming of the marauding animal from the shattered circus car. Probably, Ruth told herself before the evening was half over, "Rival's Circus and Menagerie" had moved on with all its beasts.

Uncle Jabez, however, got down the double-barreled shotgun, cleaned and oiled it, and slipped in two cartridges loaded with big shot.

"I ain't aimin' to lose my pigs if I can help it," he said.

As the evening dragged by, they all forgot the panther scare. Jerry had fallen asleep after supper without recourse to the medicine Dr. Davison had left. As usual, Uncle Jabez was poring over his daybook and counting the cash in the japanned money box.

Ruth was deep in her text books. One does forget so much between June and September! Aunt Alvirah was busily sewing some ruffled garment for "her pretty."

Suddenly a quick, stern voice spoke out of the guest room down the hall.

"Quick! bring that gun!"

Alice B. Emerson

"Hul-*lo*!" murmured Uncle Jabez, looking up.

"That poor boy's delirious," declared Aunt Alvirah.

But Ruth jumped up and ran lightly to the room where Jerry Sheming lay.

"What *is* it?" she gasped, peering at the flushed face that was raised from the pillow.

"That cat!" muttered Jerry.

"Oh, you're dreaming!" declared Ruth, trying to laugh.

"I ain't lived in the woods for nothin'," snapped the young fellow. "I never see that black panther in her native wilds, o' course; but I've tracked other kinds o' cats. And one of the tribe is 'round here—There! hear that?"

One of the horses in the stable squealed suddenly—a scream of fear. Then a cow bellowed.

Uncle Jabez came with a rush, in his stocking feet, with the heavy shotgun in his hand.

"What's up?" he demanded, hoarsely.

"I am!" exclaimed Jerry, swinging his legs out of bed, despite the pain it caused him. "Put out that light, Miss Ruth."

Aunt Alvirah hobbled in, groaning, "Oh, my back! and oh, my bones!"

Uncle Jabez softly raised the sash where the blind was missing.

"I saw her eyes," gasped Jerry, much excited. He reached out a grasping hand. "Gimme that gun, sir, unless you are a good shot. I don't often miss."

"You take it," muttered Uncle Jabez, thrusting the gun into the young fellow's hand. "My—my eyes ain't what they once was."

"Send the women folk back. If she leaps in at the winder—"

Suddenly he raised the gun to his shoulder. It was so dark in the room they all saw the crouching creature on the lawn outside. It was headed for the open window, and its eyes gleamed like yellow coals.

In a moment the gun spoke—one long tongue of flame, followed by the other, flashed into the night. There was a yowl, a struggle on the grass outside, and then—

"You're something of a shot, you be, young feller!" boomed out Jabez Potter's rough voice. "I was some mistaken in you. Ah! it hurt ye, eh?" and he proceeded to lift the suffering Jerry back into bed as tenderly as he would have handled Ruth herself.

They did not go out to see the dead panther until daybreak. Then they learned that the pair of lions had already been caught by their owners.

CHAPTER IV

ON THE WAY TO BRIARWOOD

If anything had been needed to interest Ruth Fielding deeply in the young fellow who had been injured at the scene of the railroad wreck, the occurrence that evening at the Red Mill would have provided it.

It was not enough for her to make a veritable hero of him to Helen, and Jane Ann, and Tom, when they came over from Outlook the following morning. When the girl of the Red Mill was really interested in anything or anybody, she gave her whole-souled attention to it.

She could not be satisfied with Jerry Sheming's brief account of his life with his half-crazed uncle on some distant place called Cliff Island, and the domestic tragedy that seemed to be the cause of the old man's final incarceration in a madhouse.

"Tell me all about yourself—do," she pleaded with Jerry, who was to remain in bed for several days (Uncle Jabez insisted on it himself, too!), for the injured leg must be rested. "Didn't you live anywhere else but in the woods?"

"That's right, Miss," he said, slowly. "I got a little schooling on the mainland; but it warn't much. Uncle Pete used to guide around parties of city men who wanted to fish and hunt. At the last I did most of the guidin'. He said he could trust me, for I hated liquor as bad as him. *My* dad was killed by it.

"Uncle Pete was a mite cracked over it, maybe. But he was good enough to me until Rufus Blent came rummagin' round. Somehow he got Uncle Pete to ragin'."

"Who is this Rufus Blent?" asked Ruth, curiously.

"He's a real estate man. He lives at Logwood. That's the landin' at the east end o' the lake."

"What lake?"

"Tallahaska. You've heard tell on't?" he asked.

"Yes. But I was never there, of course."

"Well, Miss, Cliff Island is just the purtiest place! And Uncle Pete must have had some title to it, for he's lived there all his life—and he's old. Fifty-odd year he was there, I know. He was more than a squatter.

"I reckon he was a bit of a miser. He had some money, and he didn't trust to banks. So he kept it hid on the island, of course.

"Then the landslide come, and he talked as though it had covered his treasure box—and in it was papers he talked about. If he could ha' got those papers he could ha' beat Rufus Blent off.

"That's the understandin' I got of him. Of course, he talked

Alice B. Emerson

right ragin' and foolish; but some things he said was onderstandable. But he couldn't make the judge see it—nor could I. They let Rufus Blent have his way, and Uncle Pete went to the 'sylum.

"Then they ordered me off the island. I believe Blent wanted to s'arch it himself for the treasure box. He's a sneakin' man—I allus hated him," said Jerry, clenching his fist angrily.

"But they could ha' put me in the jug if I'd tried to fight him. So I come away. Don't 'spect I'll ever see Tallahaska—or Cliff Island—again," and the young fellow's voice broke and he turned his face away.

When Jane Ann Hicks heard something of this, through Ruth, she was eager to help Jerry to be revenged upon the man whom he thought had cheated his uncle.

"Let me write to Bill Hicks about it," she cried, eagerly. "He'll come on here and get after this thieving real estate fellow—you bet!"

"I have no doubt that he would," laughed Helen, pinching her. "You'd make him leave his ranch and everything else and come here just to do that. Don't be rash, young lady. Jerry certainly did you a favor, but you needn't take everything he says for the gospel truth."

"I believe myself he's honest," added Ruth, quietly.

"And I don't doubt him either," Helen Cameron said. "But we'd better hear both sides of it. And a missing treasure box, and papers to prove that an old hunter is owner of an island in Tallahaska, sounds—well, unusual, to say the least."

Ruth laughed. "Helen has suddenly developed caution," she said. "What do you say, Tom?"

"I'll get father to write to somebody at Logwood, and find out about it," returned the boy, promptly.

That is the way the matter was left for the time being. The next day they were to start for school—the girls for Briarwood and Tom for Seven Oaks.

It was arranged that Jerry should remain at the Red Mill for a time. Uncle Jabez's second opinion of him was so favorable that the miller might employ him for a time as the harvesting and other fall work came on. And Jane Ann left a goodly sum in the miller's hands for young Sheming's use.

"He's that independent that he wouldn't take nothing from me but a pair of cuff links," declared Jane Ann, wiping her eyes, for she was a tender-hearted girl under her rough exterior. "Says they will do for him to remember me by. He's a nice chap."

"Jinny's getting sentimental," gibed Tom, slily.

"I'm not over you, Mister Tom!" she flared up instantly. "You're too 'advanced' a dresser."

"And you were the girl who once ran away from Silver Ranch and the boys out there, because everything was so 'common,'" chuckled Tom.

Ruth shut him off at that. She knew that the western girl could not stand much teasing.

They were all nervous, anyway; at least, the girls were. Ruth and Helen approached their second year at Briarwood with some anxiety. How would they be treated? How would the studies be arranged for the coming months of hard work? How were they going to stand with the teachers?

When the two chums first went to Briarwood they occupied a double room; but later they had taken in Mercy Curtis, a lame girl. Now that "triumvirate" could not continue, for Jane Ann had begged to room with Ruth and Helen.

The western girl, who was afraid of scarcely anything "on four legs or two" in her own environment, was really nervous as she approached boarding school. She had seen enough of these eastern girls to know that they were entirely different from herself. She was "out of their class," she told herself, and if she had not been with Ruth and Helen these few last days before the opening of the school term, she would have run away.

Ruth was going back to school this term with a delightful sense of having gained Uncle Jabez's special approval. He admitted that schooling such as she gained at Briarwood was of some use. And he made her a nice present of pocket-money when she started.

The Cameron auto stopped for her at the Red Mill before mid-forenoon, and Ruth bade the miller and Aunt Alvirah and Ben—not forgetting Jerry Sheming, her new friend—good-bye.

"Do—*do* take care o' yourself, my pretty," crooned Aunt Alvirah over her, at the last. "Jest remember we're a-honin' for you here at the ol' mill."

"Take care of Uncle Jabez," whispered Ruth. She dared kiss the grim old man only upon his dusty cheek. Then she shook hands with bashful Ben and ran out to her waiting friends.

"Come on, or we'll lose the train," cried Helen.

They were off the moment Ruth stepped into the tonneau. But she stood up and waved her hand to the little figure of Aunt Alvirah in the cottage doorway as long as she could be seen on the Cheslow road. And she had a fancy that Uncle Jabez himself was lurking in the dark opening to the grist-floor of the mill, and watching the retreating motor car.

There was a quick, alert-looking girl hobbling on two canes up and down the platform at Cheslow Station. This was Mercy Curtis, the station agent's crippled daughter.

"Here you are at last!" she cried, shrilly. "And the train already hooting for the station. Five minutes more and you would have been too late. Did you think I could go to Briarwood without you?"

Ruth ran up and kissed her heartily. She knew that Mercy's "bark was worse than her bite."

"You come and see Jane Ann—and be nice to her. She doesn't look it, but she's just as scared as she can be."

"Of course you'd have some poor, unfortunate pup, or kitten, to mother, Ruth Fielding," snapped the lame girl.

She was very nice, however, to the girl from Silver Ranch, sat beside her in the chair car, and soon had Jane Ann laughing. For Mercy Curtis, with her sarcastic tongue, could be good fun if she wished to be.

Here and there, along the route to Osago Lake, other Briarwood girls joined them. At one point appeared Madge Steele and her brother, Bob, a slow, smiling young giant, called "Bobbins" by the other boys, who was always being "looked after" in a most distressing fashion by his sister.

"Come, Bobby, boy, don't fall up the steps and get your nice new clothes dirty," adjured Madge, as her brother made a false step in getting aboard the train. "Will you look out for him, Mr. Cameron, if I leave him in your care?"

"Sure!" said Tom, laughing. "I'll see that he doesn't spoil his pinafore or mess up his curls."

"Say! I'd shake a sister like that if I had one," grunted "Busy Izzy" Phelps, disgustedly.

"Aw, what's the odds?" drawled good-natured Bobbins.

The hilarious crowd boarded the *Lanawaxa* at the landing, and after crossing the lake they again took a train, disembarking at Seven Oaks, where the boys' school was situated.

From here the girls were to journey by stage to Briarwood. There was dust-coated, grinning, bewhiskered "Old Noah Dolliver" and his "Ark," waiting for them.

There was a horde of uniformed academy boys about to greet Tom and his chums, and to eye the girls who had come thus far in their company. But Ruth and her friends were not so bashful as they had been the year before.

They formed in line, two by two, and slowly paraded the length of the platform, chanting in unison the favorite "welcome to the infants" used at the beginning of each half at Briarwood:

"Uncle Noah, he drove an Ark—
One wide river to cross!
He's aiming to land at Briarwood Park—

One wide river to cross!
One wide river!
One wide river of Jordan!
One wide river!
One wide river to cross!"

The boys cheered them enthusiastically. The girls piled into the coach with much laughter. Even Mercy had taken part in this fun, for the procession had marched at an easy pace for her benefit.

Old Dolliver cracked his whip. Tom ran along in the dust on one side and Bobbins on the other, each to bid a last good-bye to his sister.

Then the coach rolled into the shadow of the cool wood road, and Ruth and her friends were really upon the last lap of their journey to the Hall.

CHAPTER V

A LONG LOOK AHEAD

"Hurrah! first glimpse of the old place!"

Helen cried this, with her head out of the Ark. The dust rolled up in a cloud behind them as they topped the hill. Here Mary Cox had met Ruth and Helen that first day, a year ago, when they approached the Hall.

There was no infant in the coach now save Jane Ann. And the chums were determined to save the western girl from that strange and lonely feeling they had themselves experienced.

There was nobody in view on the pastured hill. Down the slope the Ark coasted and bye and bye Cedar Walk came into view.

"Shall we get out here, girls?" called Madge Steele, with a glance at Mercy.

"Of course we shall," cried that sprightly person, shaking her fist at the big senior. "Don't you dare try to spare *me*, Miss! I am getting so strong and healthy I am ashamed of myself. Don't you dare!"

Madge kissed her warmly, as Ruth had. *That* was the best way to treat Mercy Curtis whenever she "exploded."

Suddenly Helen leaned out of the open half of the door on her side and began to call a welcome to four girls who were walking briskly down the winding pathway. Instantly they began to run, shouting joyfully in return.

"Here we be, young ladies," croaked Old Dolliver, bringing his tired horses to a halt.

They struggled forth, Jane Ann coming last to help the lame girl—just a mite. Then the two parties of school friends came together like the mingling of waters.

One was a very plump girl with a smiling, rosy face; one was red-haired and very sharp-looking, and the other two balanced each other evenly, both being more than a little pretty, very well dressed, and one dark while the other was light.

The light girl was Belle Tingley, and the dark one Lluella Fairfax; of course, the red-haired one was Mary Cox, "The Fox," while the stout girl could be no other than "Heavy" Jennie Stone.

The Fox came forward quickly and seized both of Ruth's hands. "Dear Ruth," she whispered. "I arrived just this morning myself. You know that my brother is all right again?" and she kissed the girl of the Red Mill warmly.

Belle and Lluella looked a bit surprised at Mary Cox's manifestation of friendship for Ruth; but they did not yet know all the particulars of their schoolmates' adventures at Silver Ranch.

Alice B. Emerson

Heavy was hurrying about, kissing everybody indiscriminately, and of course performing this rite with Ruth at least twice.

"I'm so tickled to see you all, I can't tell!" she laughed. "And you're all looking fine, too. But it does seem a month, instead of a week, since I saw you."

"My! but you are looking bad yourself, Heavy," gibed Helen Cameron, shaking her head and staring at the other girl. "You're just fading away to a shadow."

"Pretty near," admitted Heavy. "But the doctor says I shall get my appetite back after a time. I was allowed to drink the water two eggs were boiled in for lunch, and to-night I can eat the holes out of a dozen doughnuts. Oh! I'm convalescing nicely, thank you."

The girls who had reached the school first welcomed Jane Ann quite as warmly as they did the others. There was an air about them all that seemed protecting to the strange girl.

Other girls were walking up and down the Cedar Walk, and sometimes they cast more than glances at the eight juniors who were already such friends. Madge had immediately been swallowed up by a crowd of seniors.

"Say, Foxy! got an infant there?" demanded one girl.

"I suppose Fielding has made her a Sweetbriar already—eh?" suggested another.

"The Sweetbriars do not have to fish for members," declared Helen, tossing her head.

"Oh, my! See what a long tail our cat's got!" responded one

of the other crowd, tauntingly.

"The double quartette! There's just eight of them," crowed another. "There certainly will be something doing at Briarwood Hall with those two roomsful."

"Say! that's right!" cried Heavy, eagerly, to Ruth. "You, and Helen, and Mercy, and Jinny, take that quartette room on our other side. We'll just about boss that dormitory. What do you say?"

"If Mrs. Tellingham will agree," said Ruth. "I'll ask her."

"But you girls will be 'way ahead of me in your books," broke in Jane Ann.

"We needn't be ahead of you in sleeping, and in fun," laughed Heavy, pinching her.

"Don't be offish, Miss Jinny," said Helen, calling her by the title that the cowboys did.

"And my name—my dreadful, dreadful name!" groaned the western girl.

"I tell you!" exclaimed Ruth, "we're all friends. Let's agree how we shall introduce Miss Hicks to the bunch. She must choose a name—"

"Why, call yourself 'Nita,' if you want to, dear," said Helen, patting the western girl's arm. "That's the name you ran away with."

"But I'm ashamed of that. I know it is silly—and I chose it for a silly reason. But you know what all these girls will do to 'Jane Ann,'" and she shook her head, more than a

Alice B. Emerson

little troubled.

"What's the matter with Ann?" demanded Mercy Curtis, sharply. "Isn't 'Ann Hicks' sensible-sounding enough? For sure, it's not *pretty*; but we can't all have both pretty names and pretty features," and she laughed.

"And it's mighty tough when you haven't got either." grumbled the new girl.

"'Ann Hicks,'" quoth Ruth, softly. "I like it. I believe it sounds nice, too—when you get used to it. 'Ann Hicks.' Something dignified and fine about it—just as though you had been named after some really great woman—some leader."

The others laughed; and yet they looked appreciation of Ruth Fielding's fantasy.

"Bully for you, Ruthie!" cried Helen, hugging her. "If Ann Hicks agrees."

"It doesn't sound so bad without the 'Jane,'" admitted the western girl with a sigh. "And Ruth says it so nicely."

"We'll all say it nicely," declared The Fox, who was a much different "Fox" from what she had been the year before. "'Ann Hicks,' I bet you've got a daguerreotype at home of the gentle old soul for whom you are named. You know—silver-gray gown, pearls, pink cheeks, and a real ostrich feather fan."

"My goodness me!" ejaculated the newly christened Ann Hicks, "you have already arranged a very fanciful family tree for me. Can I ever live up to such an ancestress as *that*?"

"Certainly you can," declared Ruth, firmly. "You've just *got* to. Think of the original Ann—as Mary described her—whenever you feel like exploding. Her picture ought to bring you up short. A lady like that *couldn't* explode."

"Tough lines," grumbled the western girl. "Right from what you girls call the 'wild and woolly,' and to have to live up to silver-gray silk and pearls—M-m-m-m!"

"Now, say! say!" cried Belle Tingley, suddenly, and seizing upon Ruth, about whom she had been hovering ever since they had met. "*I* want to talk a little. There aren't any more infants to christen, I hope?"

"Go on!" laughed Ruth, squeezing her. "What is the matter, *Bella mia*?"

"And don't talk Italian," said Belle, shrugging her shoulders. "Listen! I promised to ask you the minute you arrived, Ruthie, and now you've been here ten at least."

"It is something splendid," laughed Lluella, clapping her hands, evidently being already a sharer in Belle's secret.

"I'll tell you—if they'll let me," panted Belle, shaking Ruth a little. "Father's bought Cliff Island. It's a splendid place. We were there for part of the summer. And there will be a great lodge built by Christmas time and he has told me I might invite you all to come to the house-warming. Now, Ruth! it remains with you. If you'll go, the others will, I know. And it's a splendid place."

"Cliff Island?" gasped Ruth.

"Yes. In Lake Tallahaska."

Alice B. Emerson

"And your father has just bought it?"

"Yes. He had some trouble getting a clear title; but it's all right now. They had to evict an old squatter. I want you all to come with me for the mid-winter holiday. What do you say, Ruthie?" asked Belle, eagerly.

"I say it's a long look ahead," responded Ruth, slowly. "It's very kind of you, Belle. But I'll have to write home first, of course. I'd like to go, though—to Cliff Island—yes, indeed!"

CHAPTER VI

PICKING UP THE THREADS

Ann Hicks must see the preceptress at once. That came first, and Ruth would not go into the old dormitory until the introduction of the western girl was accomplished.

There was a whole bevy of girls on the steps of the main building, in which Mrs. Grace Tellingham and Dr. Tellingham lived. Nobody ever thought of putting the queer old doctor first, although all the Briarwoods respected the historian immensely. He was considered very, very scholarly, although it would have been hard to find any of his histories in any library save that of Briarwood itself.

It was understood that just now he was engaged upon a treatise relating to the possible existence of a race before the Mound Builders in the Middle West, and he was not to be disturbed, of course, at his work.

But when Ruth and Ann Hicks entered the big office room, there he was, bent over huge tomes upon the work table, his spectacles awry, and his wig pushed so far back upon his head that two hands' breadth of glistening crown was exposed.

Alice B. Emerson

The fiction that Dr. Tellingham was not bald might have been kept up very well indeed, did not the gentleman get so excited while he worked. As soon as he became interested in his books, he proceeded to bare his high brow to all beholders, and the wig slid toward the back of his neck.

The truth was, as Heavy Stone said, Dr. Tellingham had to remove his collar to brush his hair—there really was so little of it.

"Dear, dear!" sputtered the historian, peering at the two girls over his reading glasses. "You don't want me, of course?"

"Oh, no, Dr. Tellingham. This is a new girl. We wished to see Mrs. Tellingham," Ruth assured him.

"Quite so," he said, briskly. "She is—Ah! she comes! My dear! Two of the young ladies to see you," and instantly he was buried in his books again—that is, buried all but his shining crown.

Mrs. Tellingham was a graceful, gray-haired lady, with a charming smile. She trailed her black robe across the carpet and stooped to kiss Ruth warmly, for she not only respected the junior, but had learned to love her.

"Welcome, Miss Fielding!" she said, kindly. "I am glad to see you back. And this is the girl I have been getting letters about—Miss Hicks?"

"Ann Hicks," responded Ruth, firmly. "That is the name she wishes to be known by, dear Mrs. Tellingham."

"I don't know who could be writing you but Uncle Bill," said Ann Hicks, blunderingly. "And I expect he's told you a-plenty."

"I think 'Uncle Bill' must be the most recklessly generous man in the world, my dear," observed Mrs. Tellingham, taking and holding one of Ann's brown hands, and looking closely at the western girl.

For a moment the new girl blushed and her own eyes shone. "You bet he is! I—I beg pardon," she stammered. "Uncle Bill is all right."

"And Jennie Stone's Aunt Kate has been writing me about you, too. It seems she was much interested in you when you visited their place at Lighthouse Point."

"She's very kind," murmured the new girl.

"And Mrs. Murchiston, Helen's governess, has spoken a good word for you," added the preceptress.

"Why—why I didn't know so many people *cared*," stammered Ann.

"You see, you have a way of making friends unconsciously. I can see that," Mrs. Tellingham said, kindly. "Now, do not be discouraged. You will make friends among the girls in just the same way. Don't mind their banter for a while. The rough edges will soon rub off—"

"But there *are* rough edges," admitted the western girl, hanging her head.

"Don't mind. There are such in most girls' characters and they show up when first they come to school. Keep cheerful. Come to me if you are in real trouble—and stick close to Miss Fielding, here. I can't give you any better advice than that," added Mrs. Tellingham, with a laugh.

Alice B. Emerson

Then she was ready to listen to Ruth's plea that the room next to The Fox and her chums be given up to Ruth, Helen, Mercy and the new girl.

"We love our little room; but it was crowded with Mercy last half; and we could all get along splendidly in a quartette room," said Ruth.

"All right," agreed the principal. "I'll telephone to Miss Scrimp and Miss Picolet. Now, go and see about getting settled, young ladies. I expect much of you this half, Ruth Fielding. As for Ann, I shall take her in hand myself on Monday and see what classes she would best enter."

"She's fine," declared Ann Hicks, when they were outside again. "I can get along with her. But how about the girls?"

"They'll be nice to you, too—after a bit. Of course, everybody new has to expect some hazing. Thank your stars that you won't have to be put through the initiation of the marble harp," and she pointed to a marble figure in the tiny Italian garden in the middle of the campus.

When Ann wanted to know what *that* meant, Ruth repeated the legend as all new girls at Briarwood must learn it. But Ruth and her friends had long since agreed that no other nervous or high-strung girl was to be hazed, as she and Helen had been, when they first came to the Hall. So the ceremony of the marble harp was abolished. It has been described in the former volume of this series, "Ruth Fielding at Briarwood Hall."

The two went back to the dormitory that had become like home to Ruth. Miss Picolet, the little French teacher, beckoned them into her study. "I must be the good friend of your good friend, too, Miss Fielding," she said, and shook hands warmly with Ann.

The matron of the house had already opened and aired the large room next to that which had been so long occupied by The Fox and her chums. The eight girls made the corridor ring with laughter and shouts while they were getting settled. The trunks had arrived from Lumberton and Helen and Ruth were busy decorating the big room which they were to share in the future with the lame girl and Ann Hicks.

There were two wide beds in it; but each girl had her own dressing case and her locker and closet There were four windows and two study tables. It was a delightful place, they all agreed.

"Hush! tell it not in Gath; whisper it not in Ascalon!" hissed The Fox, peering into the room. "You girls have the best there is. It's lots bigger than our quartette—"

"Oh, I don't think so. Only a 'teeny' bit larger," responded Ruth, quickly.

"Then it's Heavy that takes up so much space in our room. She dwarfs everything. However," said the red-haired girl, "you can have lots more fun in here. Shove back everything against one wall, roll up the rugs, and then we can dance."

"And have Picolet after us in a hurry," observed Helen, laughing.

"Barefoot dancing is still in vogue," retorted The Fox. "Helen can play her violin."

"After retiring bell? No, thanks!" exclaimed Ruth's chum. "I am to stand better in my classes this half than last spring or Monsieur Pa-*pa* will have something to say to me. He doesn't often preach; but that black-haired brother of mine did better last term than I did. Can't have that."

"They're awfully strict with the boys over at Seven Oaks," sighed Heavy, who was chewing industriously as she talked, sitting cross-legged on the floor.

"What are you eating, Heavy?" demanded Belle, suddenly.

"Some of those doughnut holes, I bet!" giggled Lluella. "They must be awful filling, Heavy."

"Nothing *is* filling," replied the stout girl. "Just think, almost the whole universe is filled with just atmosphere—and your head, Lluella."

"That's not pretty, dear," remarked The Fox, pinching Heavy. "Don't be nasty to your playmates."

"Well, I've got to eat," groaned Heavy. "If you knew how long it seemed from luncheon to supper time—"

Despite all Ruth Fielding could do, the girl from Silver Ranch felt herself a good deal out of this nonsense and joviality. Ann could not talk the way these girls did. She felt serious when she contemplated her future in the school.

"I'd—I'd run away if it wasn't for Uncle Bill," she whispered to herself, looking out of the window at the hundreds of girls parading the walks about the campus.

Almost every two girls seemed chums. They walked with their arms about each other's waists, and chattered like magpies. Ann Hicks wanted to run and hide somewhere, for she was more lonely now than she had ever been when wandering about the far-reaching range on the Montana ranch!

CHAPTER VII

"A HARD ROW TO HOE"

Since Ruth Fielding had organized the S.B.'s, or Sweetbriars, there had been little hazing at Briarwood Hall. Of course, this was the first real opening of the school year since that auspicious occasion; but the effect of the new society and its teachings upon the whole school was marked.

Rivalries had ceased to a degree. The old Upedes, of which The Fox had been the head, no longer played their tricks. The Fox had grown much older in appearance, if not in years. She had had her lesson.

Belle and Lluella and Heavy were not so reckless, either. And as the S.B.'s stood for friendship, kindness, helpfulness, and all its members wore the pretty badge, it was likely to be much easier for those "infants" who joined the school now.

Ann Hicks was bound to receive some hard knocks, even as Mrs. Tellingham had suggested. But "roughing it" a little is sometimes good for girls as well as boys.

In her own western home Ann could have held her own with anybody. She was so much out of her usual element here at Briarwood that she was like a startled hare. She scented

Alice B. Emerson

danger on all sides.

Her roommates could not always defend her, although even Mercy, the unmerciful, tried. Ann Hicks was so big, and blundering. She was taller than most girls of her age, and "raw-boned" like her uncle. Some time she might really be handsome; but there was little promise of it as yet.

When the principal started her in her studies, it was soon discovered that Ann, big girl though she was, had to take some of the lessons belonging to the primary grade. And she made a sorry appearance in recitation, at best.

There were plenty of girls to laugh at her. There is nothing so cruel as a schoolgirl's tongue when it is unbridled. And unless the victim is blessed with either a large sense of humor, or an apt brain for repartee, it goes hard with her.

Poor Ann had neither—she was merely confused and miserable.

She saw the other girls of her room—and their close friends in the neighboring quartette—going cheerfully about the term's work. They had interests that the girl from the West, with her impoverished mind, could not even appreciate.

She had to study so hard—even some of the simplest lessons —that she had little time to learn games. She did not care for gymnasium work, although there were probably few girls at the school as muscular as herself. Tennis seemed silly to her. Nobody rode at the Hall, and she longed to bestride a pony and dash off for a twenty-mile canter.

Nothing that she was used to doing on the ranch would appeal to these girls here—Ann was quite sure of that. Ruth and the others who had been with them for that all-too-short month at Silver Ranch seemed to have forgotten the riding, and the roping, and all.

Then, Helen had her violin—and loved it. Ruth was practicing singing all the time she could spare, for she was already a prominent member of the Glee Club. When the girl of the Red Mill sang, Ann Hicks felt her heart throb and the tears rise in her eyes. She loved Ruth's kind of music; yet she, herself, could not carry a tune.

Mercy was strictly attentive to her own books. Mercy was a bookworm—nor did she like being asked questions about her studies. Those first few weeks Ann Hicks's recitations did not receive very high marks.

Often some of the girls who did not know her very well laughed because she carried books belonging to the primary grade. Ann Hicks had many studies to make up that her mates had been drilled in while they were in the lower classes.

One day at mail time (and in a boarding school that is a most important hour) Ann received a very tempting-looking box by parcel post. She had been initiated into the meaning of "boxes from home." Even Aunt Alvirah had sent a box to Ruth, filled with choicest homemade dainties.

Ann expected nothing like that. Uncle Bill would never think of it—and he wouldn't know what to buy, anyway. The box fairly startled the girl from Silver Ranch.

"What is it? Something good to eat, I bet," cried Heavy, who was on hand, of course. "Open it, Ann—do."

"Come on! Let's see what the goodies are," urged another girl, but who smiled behind her hand.

Alice B. Emerson

"I don't know who would send *me* anything," said Ann, slowly.

"Never mind the address. Open it!" cried a third speaker, and had Ann noted it, she would have realized that some of the most trying girls in the school had suddenly surrounded her.

With trembling fingers she tore off the outside wrapper without seeing that the box had been mailed at the local post office—Lumberton!

A very decorative box was enclosed.

"H-m-m!" gasped Heavy. "Nothing less than fancy nougatines in *that*."

She was aiding the heartless throng, but did not know it. It would have never entered Heavy's mind to do a really mean thing.

Ann untied the narrow red ribbon. She raised the cover. Tissue paper covered something very choice—?

A dunce cap.

For a moment Ann was stricken motionless. The girls about her shouted. One coarse, thoughtless girl seized the cap, pulled it from the box, and clapped it on Ann Hicks's black hair.

The delighted crowd shouted more shrilly. Heavy was thunderstruck. Then she sputtered:

"Well! I never would have believed there was anybody so mean as that in the whole of Briarwood School."

But Ann, who had held in her temper as she governed a half-wild pony on the range, until this point, suddenly "let go all holts," as Bill Hicks would have expressed it.

She tore the cap from her head and stamped upon it and the fancy box it had come in. She struck right and left at the laughing, scornful faces of the girls who had so baited her.

Had it not been disgraceful, one might have been delighted with the change in the expression of those faces—and in the rapidity with which the change came about.

More than one blow landed fairly. The print of Ann's fingers was impressed in red upon the cheeks of those nearest to her. They ran screaming—some laughing, some angry.

Heavy's weight (for the fleshy girl had seized Ann about the waist) was all that made the enraged girl give over her pursuit of her tormentors. Fortunately, Ruth herself came running to the spot. She got Ann away and sat by her all the afternoon in their room, making up her own delinquent lessons afterward.

But the affair could not be passed over without comment. Some of the girls had reported Ann's actions. Of course, such a disgraceful thing as a girl slapping another was seldom heard of in Briarwood. Mrs. Tellingham, who knew very well where the blame lay, dared not let the matter go without punishing Ann, however.

"I am grieved that one of our girls—a young lady in the junior grade—should so forget herself," said the principal. "Whatever may have been the temptation, such an exhibition of temper cannot be allowed. I am sure she will not yield to it again; nor shall I pass leniently over the person who may again be the cause of Ann Hicks losing her temper."

Alice B. Emerson

This seemed to Ann to be "the last straw." "She might have better put me in the primary grade in the beginning," the ranch girl said, spitefully. "Then I wouldn't have been among those who despise me. I hate them all! I'll just get away from here—"

But the thought of running away a second time rather troubled her. She had worried her uncle greatly the first time she had done so. Now he was sure she was in such good hands that she wouldn t wish to run away.

Ann knew that she could not blame Ruth Fielding, and the other girls who were always kind to her. She merely shrank from being with them, when they knew so much more than she did.

It was her pride that was hurt. Had she taken the teasing of the meaner girls in a wiser spirit, she knew they would not have sent her the dunce cap. They continued to tease her because they knew they could hurt her.

"I—I wish I could show them I could do things that they never dreamed of doing!" muttered Ann, angrily, yet wistfully, too. "I'd like to fling a rope, or manage a bad bronc', or something they never saw a girl do before.

"Book learning isn't everything. Oh! I have half a mind to give up and go back to the ranch. Nobody made fun of me out there—they didn't dare! And our folks are too kind to tease that way, anyhow," thought the western girl.

"Uncle Bill is just paying out his good money for nothing. He said Ruth was a little lady—and Helen, too. I knew he wanted me to be the same, after he got acquainted with them and saw how fine they were.

"But you sure 'can't make a silk purse out of a sow's ear.' That's as certain as shootin'! If I stay here I've got a mighty hard row to hoe—and—and I don't believe I've got the pluck to hoe it." Ann groaned, and shook her tousled black head.

Alice B. Emerson

CHAPTER VIII

JERRY SHEMING AGAIN

Ruth, with all the fun and study of the opening of the fall term at Briarwood, could not entirely forget Jerry Sheming. More particularly did she think of him because of the invitation Belle Tingley had extended to her the day of their arrival.

It was a coincidence that none of the other girls appreciated, for none of them had talked much with the young fellow who had saved Ann Hicks from the wrecked car at Applegate Crossing. Even Ann herself had not become as friendly with the boy as had Ruth.

The fact that he had lived a good share of his life on the very island Belle said her father had bought for a hunting camp, served to spur Ruth's interest in both the youth and the island itself. Then, what Jerry had told her about his uncle's lost treasure box added to the zest of the affair.

Somewhere on the island Peter Tilton had lost a box containing money and private papers. Jerry believed it to have been buried by a landslide that had occurred months before.

There must be something in this story, or why should "Uncle Pete," as Jerry called him, have lost his mind over the catastrophe? Uncle Pete must be really mad or they would not have shut him up in the county asylum.

The loss of the papers supposed to be in the box made it possible for some man named Blent to cheat the old hunter out of his holdings on Cliff Island.

Not for a moment did Ruth suppose that Mr. Tingley, Belle's father, was a party to any scheme for cheating the old hunter. It was the work of the man Blent—if true.

Ruth was very curious—and very much interested. Few letters ever passed between her and the Red Mill. Aunt Alvirah's gnarled and twisted fingers did not take kindly to the pen; and Uncle Jabez loved better to add up his earnings than to spend an evening retailing the gossip of the Mill for his grandniece to peruse.

Ruth knew that Jerry had soon recovered from his accident and that for several weeks, at least, had worked for Uncle Jabez. The latter grudgingly admitted that Jerry was the best man he had ever hired in the cornfield, both in cutting fodder and shucking corn.

Just before Thanksgiving there came a letter saying that Jerry had gone on. Of course, Ruth knew that her uncle would not keep the young fellow longer than he could make use of him; but she was sorry he had gone before she had communicated with him.

The girl of the Red Mill felt that she wished to know Jerry better. She had been deeply interested in his story. She had hoped to learn more about him.

Alice B. Emerson

"If you are really going to Cliff Island for the holidays, Belle," she told the latter, "I hope I can go."

"Bully!" exclaimed Belle, joyfully. "We'll have a dandy time there—better than we had at Helen's father's camp, last winter. I refuse to be lost in the snow again."

"Same here," drawled Heavy. "But I wish that lake you talk about, Belle, wouldn't freeze over. I don't like ice," with a shiver.

"Who ever heard of water that wouldn't freeze?" demanded Belle, scornfully.

"I have," said Heavy, promptly.

"What kind of water, I'd like to know, Miss?"

"Hot water," responded Heavy, chuckling.

Helen, and most of the other girls who were invited to Cliff Island for Christmas, had already accepted the invitation. Ruth wrote to her uncle with some little doubt. She did not know how he would take the suggestion. She had been at the mill so little since first she began attending boarding school.

This Thanksgiving she did not expect to go home. Few of the girls did so, for the recess was only over the week-end and lessons began again on Monday. Only those girls who lived very near to Briarwood made a real vacation of the first winter holiday. A good many used the time to make up lessons and work off "conditions."

Thanksgiving Day itself was made somewhat special by a trip to Buchane Falls, where there was a large dam. Dinner was to be served at five in the evening, and more than half the school went off to the falls (which was ten miles away) in several big party wagons, before ten o'clock in the morning.

"Bring your appetites back with you, girls," Mrs. Tellingham told them at chapel, and Heavy, at least, had promised to do so and meant to keep her word. Yet even Heavy did justice to the cold luncheon that was served to all of them at the falls.

It was crisp autumn weather. Early in the morning there had been a skim of ice along the edge of the water; but there had not yet been frost enough to chain the current of the Buchane Creek. Indeed, it would not freeze over in the middle until mid-winter, if then.

The picnic ground was above the falls and on the verge of the big millpond. There were swings, and a bowling alley, and boats, and other amusements.

Ruth had fairly dragged Ann Hicks into the party. The girls who had been meanest to the westerner were present. Ann would have had a woefully bad time of it had not some of the smaller girls needed somebody to look out for them.

Ann hated the little girls at Briarwood less than she did the big ones. In fact, the "primes," as they were called, rather took to the big girl from the West.

One of the swings was not secure, and Ann started to fix it. She could climb like any boy, and there did not happen to be a teacher near to forbid her. Therefore, up she went, unfastened the rope from the beam, and proceeded to splice the place where it had become frayed.

It was not a new rope, but was strong save in that one spot.

Alice B. Emerson

Ann coiled it, and although it did not have the "feel" of the fine hemp, or the good hair rope that is part of the cowman's equipment, her hands and arm tingled to lassoo some active, running object.

She coiled it once more and then flung the rope at a bush. The little girls shouted their appreciation. Ann did not mind, for there seemed to be no juniors or seniors there to see. Most of the older girls were down by the water.

Indeed, some of the seniors were trying to interest the bigger girls in rowing. Briarwood owned a small lake, and they might have canoes and racing shells upon it, if the girls as a whole would become interested.

But many of the big girls did not even know how to row. There was one big punt into which almost a dozen of them crowded. Heavy sat in the stern and declared that she had to have a big crowd in the bow of the boat, to balance it and keep her end from going down.

Therefore one girl after another jumped in, and when it was really too full for safety it was pushed out from the landing. Just about the time the current which set toward the middle of the pond seized the punt, it was discovered that nobody had thought of oars.

"How under the sun did you suppose a thing like this was going to be propelled?" Heavy demanded. "I never did see such a fellow as you are, Mandy Mitchell!"

"You needn't scold me," declared the Mitchell girl. "You invited me into the boat."

"Did I? Why! I must have been crazy, then!" declared Heavy. "And didn't any of you think how we were going to get back to shore?"

"Nor we don't know now," cried another girl.

"Oh-o!" gasped one of the others, darting a frightened look ahead. "We're aiming right for the dam."

"You wouldn't expect the boat to drift against the current, would you?" snapped Heavy.

"Let's scream!" cried another—and they could all do that to perfection. In a very few minutes it was apparent to everybody within the circle of half a mile or more that a bunch of girls was in trouble—or thought so!

"Sit down!" gasped Heavy. "Don't rock the boat. If that yelling doesn't bring anybody, we're due to reach a watery grave, sure enough."

"Oh, don't, Heavy!" wailed one of the weaker ones. "How can you?"

Heavy was privately as frightened as any of them, but she tried to keep the others cheerful, and would have kept on joking till the end. But several small boats came racing down the pond after them, and along the bank came a man—or a boy—running and shouting. How either the girls in the boats or the youth on the shore could help them, was a mystery; but both comforted the imperiled party immensely.

The current swung the heavy punt in toward the shore. Right at that end of the dam the water was running a foot deep—or more—over the flash-board.

If the punt struck, it would turn broadside, and probably tip all hands over the dam. This was a serious predicament, indeed, and the spectators realized it even more keenly than did the girls in the punt.

The youth who had been called to the spot by their screams threw off his coat and cap, and they saw him stoop to unlace his shoes. A plunge into this cold water was not attractive, and it was doubtful if he could help them much if he reached the punt.

Down the hill from the picnic grounds came a group of girls, Ann Hicks in the lead. Most of her companions were too small to do any good in any event. The girl from the ranch carried a neat coil of rope in one hand and she shouted to Heavy to "Hold on!"

"You tell me what to hold on to, and you'll see me do it!" replied the plump girl. "All I can take hold of just now is thin air."

"Hold on!" said Ann again, and stopped, having reached the right spot. Then she swung the rope in the air, let it uncoil suddenly, and the loose end dropped fairly across Jennie Stone's lap.

"Hold on!" yelled everybody, then, and Heavy obeyed.

But the young fellow sprang to Ann's aid, and wrapped the slack of the rope around a stout sapling on the edge of the pond.

"Easy! Easy!" he admonished. "We don't want to pull them out of the boat. You *can* fling a rope; can't you, Miss?"

"I'd ought to," grunted Ann. "I've roped enough steers— Why! you're Jerry Sheming," she declared, suddenly looking into his face. "Ruth Fielding wants to see you. Don't you run away before she talks with you."

Then the rope became taut, and the punt began to swing shoreward slowly, taking in some water and setting the girls to screaming again.

CHAPTER IX

RUTH'S LITTLE PLOT

The punt was in shallow water and the girls who had ventured into it without oars were perfectly safe before any of the teachers arrived. With them came Ruth and Helen, and some of the other juniors and seniors. Heavy took the stump.

"Now! you see what she did?" cried the stout girl, seizing Ann in her arms the moment she could get ashore. "If she hadn't known how to fling a lasso, and rope a steer, she'd never have been able to send that rope to us.

"Three cheers for Ann Hicks, the girl from the ranch, who knows what to do when folks are drowning in Buchane Pond! One—two—three—"

The cheers were given with a will. Several of the girls who had treated the western girl so meanly about the dunce cap had been in the boat, and they asked Ann to shake hands. They were truly repentant, and Ann could not refuse their advances.

But the western girl was still doubtful of her standing with her mates, and went back to play with the little ones. Meanwhile she showed Ruth where Jerry Sheming stood at one side, and the girl from the Red Mill ran to him eagerly.

"I am delighted to see you!" she exclaimed, shaking Jerry's rough hand. "I was afraid I wouldn't be able to find you after you left the mill. And I wanted to."

"I'm glad of your interest in me, Miss Ruth," he said, "but I ain't got no call to expect it. Mr. Potter was pretty kind to me, and he kept me as long as there was work there."

"But you haven't got to tramp it, now?"

"Only to look for a steady job. I—I come over this way hopin' I'd hit it at Lumberton. But they're discharging men at the mills instead of hiring new ones."

"And I expect you'd rather work in the woods than anywhere else?" suggested Ruth.

"Why—yes, Miss. I love the woods. And I got a good rifle and shotgun, and I'm a good camp cook. I can't get a guide's license, but I could go as assistant—if anybody would take me around Tallahaska."

"Suppose I could get you a job working right where you've always lived—at Cliff Island?" she asked, eagerly.

"What d'ye mean—Cliff Island?" he demanded, flushing deeply. "I wouldn't work for that Rufus Blent—nor he wouldn't have me."

"I don't know anything about the man," said Ruth, smiling. "But one of my chums has invited me to go to Cliff Island for the Christmas holidays. Her father has bought the place and is building a lodge there."

Alice B. Emerson

"Good lands!" ejaculated Jerry.

"Isn't that a coincidence?" Ruth commented. "Now, you wouldn't refuse a job with Mr. Tingley; would you?"

"Tingley—is that the name?"

"Yes. Perhaps I can get him, through Belle, to hire you. I'll try. Would you go back?"

"In a minute!" exclaimed Jerry.

"Then I'll try. You see, in four or five weeks, we'll be going there ourselves. I think it would just be jolly to have you around, for you know all about the island and everything."

"Yes, indeed, ma'am," agreed Jerry. "I'd like the job."

"So you must write me every few days and let me know where you are. Mrs. Tellingham won't mind—I'll explain to her," Ruth said, earnestly. "I am not quite sure that I can go myself, yet. But I'll know for sure in a few days. And I'll see if Belle won't ask her father to give you work at Cliff Island. Then, in your off time, you can look for that box your uncle lost. Don't you see?"

"Oh, Miss! I guess that's gone for good. Near as I could make out o' Uncle Pete, the landslide at the west end of the island buried his treasure box a mile deep! It was in one o' the little caves, I s'pose."

"Caves? Are there caves on the island?"

"Lots of 'em. Big ones as well as small. If Uncle Pete wasn't plumb crazy, he had his money and papers in a hide-out that I'd never found."

"I see Miss Picolet coming this way. She won't approve of my talking with 'a strange young man' so long," laughed Ruth. "You let me know every few days where you are, Jerry?"

"Yes, ma'am, I will. And thank you kindly."

"You aren't out of funds? You have money?"

"I've got quite a little store," said Jerry, smiling. "Thanks to that nice black-eyed girl that I helped out of the car window."

"Oh! Ann Hicks. And she's being made much of, now, by the girls, because she knew how to fling a rope," cried Ruth, looking across the picnic ground to where her schoolmates were grouped.

"She's all right," said Jerry, enthusiastically. "They ought to be proud of her—them that was in that boat."

"It will break the ice for Ann," declared Ruth. "I am so glad. Now, I must run. Don't forget to write, Jerry. Good bye."

She gave him her hand and ran back to join her school friends. Ann had gone about putting up the children's swing and at first had paid little attention to the enthusiasm of the girls who had been saved from going over the dam. But she could not ignore them altogether.

"You're just the smartest girl I ever saw," Heavy declaimed. "We'd all be in the water, sure enough, if you hadn't got that rope to us. Come on, Ann! Be a sport. *Do* wear your laurels kindly."

"I'm just as 'dumb' about books as ever. Flinging that rope

Alice B. Emerson

didn't make any difference," growled the western girl.

"I don't care if you don't know your 'A.B., abs,'" cried one of the girls who had taken a prominent part in the dunce cap trick. "You make me awfully ashamed of myself for being so mean to you. Please forgive us all, Ann—that's a good girl."

Ann was awkward about accepting their apologies; and yet she was not naturally a bad-tempered girl. She was just different from them all—and felt the difference so keenly!

This sudden reversal of feeling, and their evident offer of friendliness, made her feel more awkward than ever. She remained very glum while at the picnic grounds.

But, as Ruth had said, the incident served to break the ice. Ann had gotten her start. Somebody beside the "primes" gave her "the glad hand and the smiling eye." Briarwood began to be a different sort of place for the ranch girl.

There were plenty of the juniors who looked down on her still; but she had "shown them" once that she could do something the ordinary eastern girl could not do and Ann was on the *qui vive* for another chance to "make good" along her own particular line.

She grew brighter and more self-possessed as the term advanced. Her lessons, too, she attacked with more assurance.

A few days after Thanksgiving Ruth received a letter in Aunt Alvirah's cramped hand-writing which assured her that Uncle Jabez would make no objection to her accepting the invitation to go to Cliff Island for the holidays.

"And I'll remind him of it in time so't he can send you a Christmas goldpiece, if the sperit so moves him," wrote Aunt

Alvirah, in her old-fashioned way. "But do take care of your-self, my pretty, in the middle of that lake."

In telling Belle how happy she was to accept the invitation for the frolic, Ruth diffidently put forward her request that Mr. Tingley give Jerry Sheming a job.

"I am quite sure he is a good boy," she told Belle. "He has worked for my uncle, and Uncle Jabez praised him. Now, Uncle Jabez doesn't praise for nothing."

"I'll tell father about this Jerry—sure," laughed Belle. "You're an odd girl, Ruth. You're always trying to do some-thing for somebody."

"Trying to do somebody for somebody, maybe," interposed Mercy, in her sharp way. "Ruth uses her friends for her own ends."

But Ruth's little plot worked. A fortnight after Thanksgiving she was able to write to Jerry, who had found a few days' work near the school, that he could go back to Cliff Island and present himself to Mr. Tingley's foreman. A good job was waiting for him on the island where he had lived so long with his uncle, the old hunter.

CHAPTER X

AN EXCITING FINISH

Affairs at Briarwood went at high speed toward the end of the term. Everybody was busy. A girl who did not work, or who had no interest in her studies, fell behind very quickly.

Ann Hicks was spurred to do her best by the activities of her mates. She did not like any of them well enough—save those in the two neighboring quartette rooms in her dormitory building—to accept defeat from them. She began to make a better appearance in recitations, and her marks became better.

They all had extra interests save Ann herself. Helen Cameron was in the school orchestra and played first violin with a hope of getting solo parts in time. She loved the instrument, and in the evening, before the electricity was turned on, she often played in the room, delighting the music-loving Ann.

Sometimes Ruth sang to her chum's accompaniment. Ruth's voice was so sweet, so true and tender, and she sang ballads with such feeling, that Ann often was glad it was dark in the room. The western girl considered it "soft" to weep, but Ruth's singing brought the tears to her eyes.

Mercy Curtis even gave up her beloved books during the hour of these informal concerts. Other times she would have railed because she could not study. Mercy was as hungry for lessons as Heavy Stone was for layer-cake and macaroons.

"That's all that's left me," croaked the lame girl, when she was in one of her most difficult moods. "I'll learn all there is to be learned. I'll stuff my head full. Then, when other girls laugh at my crooked back and weak legs, I'll shame 'em by knowing more out of books."

"Oh, what a mean way to put it!" gasped Helen.

"I don't care, Miss! You never had your back ache you and your legs go wabbly—No person with a bad back and such aches and pains as I have, was ever good-natured!"

"Think of Aunt Alvirah," murmured Ruth, gently.

"Oh, well—she isn't just human!" gasped the lame girl.

"She is very human, I think," Ruth returned.

"No. She's an angel. And no angel was ever called 'Curtis,'" declared the other, her eyes snapping.

"But I believe there must be an angel somewhere named 'Mercy,'" Ruth responded, still softly.

However, it was understood that Mercy was aiming to be the crack scholar of her class. There was a scholarship to be won, and Mercy hoped to get it and to go to college two years later.

Even Jennie Stone declared she was going in for "extras."

Alice B. Emerson

"What, pray?" scoffed The Fox. "All your spare time is taken up in eating now, Miss."

"All right. I'll go in for the heavyweight championship at table," declared the plump girl, good-naturedly. "At least, the result will doubtless be visible."

Ann began to wonder what she was studying for. All these other girls seemed to have some particular object. Was she going to school without any real reason for it?

Uncle Bill would be proud of her, of course. She practised assiduously to perfect her piano playing. That was something that would show out in Bullhide and on the ranch. Uncle Bill would crow over her playing just as he did over her bareback riding.

But Ann was not entirely satisfied with these thoughts. Nor was she contented with the fact that she had begun to make her mates respect her. There was something lacking.

She had half a mind to refuse Belle Tingley's invitation to Cliff Island. In her heart Ann believed she was included in the party because Belle would have been ashamed to ignore her, and Ruth would not have gone had Ann not been asked.

To tell the truth Ann was hungry for the girls to like her for herself—for some attribute of character which she honestly possessed. She had never had to think of such things before. In her western home it had never crossed her mind whether people liked her, or not. Everybody about Silver Ranch had been uniformly kind to her.

Belle's holiday party was to be made up of the eight girls in the two quartette rooms, with Madge Steele, the senior; Madge's brother, Bobbins, Tom Cameron, little Busy Izzy

Phelps, and Belle's own brothers.

"Of course, we've got to have the boys," declared Helen. "No fun without them."

Mercy had tried to beg off at first; then she had agreed to go, if she could take half a trunkful of books with her.

Briarwood girls were as busy as bees in June during these last few days of the first half. The second half was broken by the Easter vacation and most of the real hard work in study came before Christmas.

There was going to be a school play after Christmas, and the parts were given out before the holidays. Helen was going to play and Ruth to sing. It did seem to Ann as though every girl was happy and busy but herself.

The last day of the term was in sight. There was to be the usual entertainment and a dance at night. The hall had to be trimmed with greens and those girls—of the junior and senior classes—who could, were appointed to help gather the decorations.

"I don't want to go," objected Ann.

"Goosie!" cried Helen. "Of course you do. It will be fun."

"Not for me," returned the ranch girl, grimly. "Do you see who is going to head the party? That Mitchell girl. She's always nasty to me."

"Be nasty to her!" snapped Mercy, from her corner.

"Now, Mercy!" begged Ruth, shaking a finger at the lame girl.

Alice B. Emerson

"I wouldn't mind what Mitchell says or does," sniffed The Fox.

"Fibber!" exclaimed Mercy.

"I never tell lies, Miss," said Mary Cox, tossing her head.

"Humph!" ejaculated the somewhat spiteful Mercy, "do you call yourself a female George Washington?"

"No. Marthy Washington," laughed Heavy.

"Only her husband couldn't lie," declared Mercy. "And at that, they say that somebody wished to change the epitaph on his tomb to read: 'Here lies George Washington—for the first time!'"

"Everybody is tempted to tell a fib some time," sighed Helen.

"And falls, too," exclaimed Mercy.

"I must say I don't believe there ever was anybody but Washington that didn't tell a lie. It's awfully hard to be exactly truthful always," said Lluella. "You remember that time in the primary grade, just after we'd come here to Briarwood, Belle?"

"Do I?" laughed Belle Tingley. "You fibbed all right then, Miss."

"It wasn't very bad—and I did *want* to see the whole school so much. So—so I took one of my pencils to our teacher and asked her if she would ask the other scholars if it was theirs.

"Of course, all the other girls in our room said it wasn't," proceeded Lluella. "Then teacher said just what I wanted her to say: 'You may inquire in the other classes.' So I went around and saw all the other classes and had a real nice time.

"But when I got back with the pencil in my hand still, Belle come near getting me into trouble."

"Uh-huh!" admitted Belle, nodding.

"How?" asked somebody.

"She just whispered—right out loud, 'Lluella, that is your pencil and you know it!' And I had to say—right off, 'It isn't, and I didn't!' Now, what could I have said else? But it was an awful fib, I s'pose."

The assembled girls laughed. But Ann Hicks was still seriously inclined not to go into the woods, although she had no idea of telling a fib about it. And because she was too proud to say to the teacher in charge that she feared Miss Mitchell's tongue, the western girl joined the greens-gathering party at the very last minute.

There were two four-seated sleighs, for there was a hard-packed white track into the woods toward Triton Lake. Old Dolliver drove one, and his helper manned the other. The English teacher was in charge. She hoped to find bushels of holly berries and cedar buds as well as the materials for wreaths.

One pair of the horses was western—high-spirited, hard-bitted mustangs. Ann Hicks recognized them before she got into the sleigh. How they pulled and danced, and tossed the froth from their bits!

"I feel just as they do," thought the girl. "I'd love to break out, and kick, and bite, and act the very Old Boy! Poor

Alice B. Emerson

things! How they must miss the plains and the free range."

The other girls wondered what made her so silent. The tang of the frosty air, and the ring of the ponies' hoofs, and the jingle of the bells put plenty of life and fun into her mates; but Ann remained morose.

They reached the edge of the swamp and the girls alighted with merry shout and song. They were all armed with big shears or sharp knives, but the berries grew high, and Old Dolliver's boy had to climb for them.

Then the accident occurred—a totally unexpected and unlooked for accident. In stepping out on a high branch, the boy slipped, fell, and came down to the ground, hitting each intervening limb, and so saving his life, but dashing every bit of breath from his lungs, it seemed!

The girls ran together, screaming. The teacher almost fainted. Old Dolliver stooped over the fallen boy and wiped the blood from his lips.

"Don't tech him!" he croaked. "He's broke ev'ry bone in his body, I make no doubt. An' he'd oughter have a doctor—"

"I'll get one," said Ann Hicks, briskly, in the old man's ear. "Where's the nearest—and the best?"

"Doc Haverly at Lumberton."

"I'll get him."

"It's six miles, Miss. You'd never walk it. I'll take one of the teams—"

"You stay with him," jerked out Ann. "I can ride."

"Ride? Them ain't ridin' hosses, Miss," declared Old Dolliver.

"If a horse has got four legs he can be ridden," declared the girl from the ranch, succinctly.

"Take the off one on my team, then—"

"That old plug? I guess not!" exclaimed Ann, and was off.

She unharnessed one of the pitching, snapping mustangs. "Whoa—easy! You wouldn't bite me, you know," she crooned, and the mustang thrust forward his ears and listened.

She dropped off the heavy harness. The bridle she allowed to remain, but there was no saddle. The English teacher came to her senses, suddenly.

"That creature will kill you!" she cried, seeing what Ann was about.

"Then he'll be the first horse that ever did it," drawled Ann. "Hi, yi, yi! We're off!"

To the horror of the teacher, to the surprise of Old Dolliver, and to the delight of the other girls, Ann Hicks swung herself astride of the dancing pony, dug her heels into his ribs, and the next moment had darted out of sight down the wood road.

Alice B. Emerson

CHAPTER XI

A NUMBER OF THINGS

There may have been good reason for the teacher to be horrified, but how else was the mustang to be ridden? Ann was a big girl to go tearing through the roads and 'way into Lumberton astride a horse. Without a saddle and curb, however, she could not otherwise have clung to him.

Just now haste was imperative. She had a picture in her mind, all the way, of that boy lying in the snow, his face so pallid and the bloody foam upon his lips.

In twenty-five minutes she was at the physician's gate. She flung herself off the horse, and as she shouted her news to the doctor through the open office window, she unbuckled the bridle-rein and made a leading strap of it.

So, when the doctor drove out of the yard in his sleigh, she hopped in beside him and led the heaving mustang back into the woods. Of course she did not look ladylike at all, and not another girl at Briarwood would have done it. But even the English teacher—who was a prude—never scolded her for it.

Indeed, the doctor made a heroine of Ann, Old Dolliver said he never saw her beat, and the boy, who was so sadly hurt (but who pulled through all right in the end) almost worshipped the girl from Silver Ranch.

"And how she can ride!" the very girl who had treated Ann the meanest said of her. "What does it matter if she isn't quite up to the average yet in recitations? She *will* be."

This was after the holidays, however. There was too short a time before Belle Tingley and her friends started for Cliff Island for Ann to particularly note the different manner in which the girls in general treated her.

The party went on the night train. Mr. Tingley, who had some influence with the railroad, had a special sleeper side-tracked at Lumberton for their accommodation. This sleeper was to be attached to the train that went through Lumberton at midnight.

Therefore they did not have to skip all the fun of the dance. This was one of the occasions when the boys from the Seven Oaks Military Academy were allowed to mix freely with the girls of Briarwood. And both parties enjoyed it.

Belle's mother had arrived in good season, for she was to chaperone the party bound for Logwood, at the head of Tallahaska Lake. She passed the word at ten o'clock, and the girls got their hand-baggage and ran down to the road, where Old Dolliver waited for them with his big sleigh. The boys walked into town, so the girls were nicely settled in the car when Tom Cameron and his chums reached the siding.

Belle Tingley's two brothers were not too old to be companions for Tom, Bob, and Isadore Phelps. And they were all as eager for fun and prank-playing as they could be.

Mrs. Tingley had already retired and most of the girls were

in their dressing gowns when the boys arrived. The porter was making up the boys' berths as the latter tramped in, bringing on their clothing the first flakes of the storm that had been threatening all the evening.

"Let the porter brush you, little boy," urged Madge, peering out between the curtains of her section and admonishing her big brother. "If you get cold and catch the croup I don't know what sister *will* do! Now, be a good child!"

"Huh!" grunted Isadore Phelps, trying to collect enough of the snow to make a ball to throw at her. "I wonder at you, Bobbins. Why don't you make her behave? Treatin' you like an over-grown kid."

"I'd never treat *you* that way, Master Isadore," said Madge, sweetly. "For you very well know that you're not grown at all!"

At that Isadore *did* gather snow—by running out for it. He brought back a dozen snowballs and the first thing the girls knew the missiles were dropping over the top of the curtains into the sheltered spaces devoted to the berths.

There *was* a great squealing then, for some of the victims were quite ready for bed, and the snow was cold and wet. Mrs. Tingley interfered little with the pranks of the young folk, and Izzy was careful not to throw any snow into *her* compartment.

But the tease did not know when to stop. He was usually that way—as Madge said, Izzy would drive a willing horse to death.

It was Heavy and Ann, however, who paid him back in some of his own coin.

The boys finally made their preparations for bed. Izzy paraded the length of the car in his big robe and bed slippers, for a drink of ice water.

Before he could return, Heavy and Ann bounced out in their woolen kimonas and seized him. By this time the train had come in, the engine had switched to the siding, picked up their sleeper, and was now backing down to couple on to the train again.

The two girls ran Izzy out into the vestibule, Heavy's hand over his mouth so that he could not shout to his friends for help. The door of the vestibule on the off side was unlocked. Ann pushed it open.

The snow was falling heavily—it was impossible to see even the fence that bounded the railroad line on this side. The cars came together with a slight shock and the three were thrown into a giggling, struggling heap on the platform.

"Lemme go!" gasped Izzy.

"Sure we will!" giggled Heavy, and with a final push she sent him flying down the steps. Then she shut the door.

She did not know that every other door on that side of the long train was locked. Almost immediately the train began to move forward. It swept away from the Lumberton platform, and it was fully a minute before Heavy and Ann realized what they had done.

"Oh, oh, oh!" shrieked the plump girl, running down the aisle. "Busy Izzy is left behind."

"Stop your joking," exclaimed Tom, peering out of his berth, which was an upper. "He's nothing of the kind."

Alice B. Emerson

"He is! He is!"

"Why, he's all ready for bed," declared one of the Tingley boys. "He wouldn't dare—"

"We threw him out!" wailed Heavy. "We didn't know the train was to start so quickly."

"Threw him off the train?" cried Mrs. Tingley, appearing in her boudoir cap and gown. "What kind of a menagerie am I supposed to preserve order in—?"

"You can make bully good preserved ginger, Ma," said one of her sons, "but you fall short when it comes to preserving *order*."

Most of the crowd were troubled over Isadore's absence. Some suggested pulling the emergency cord and stopping the train; others were for telegraphing back from the next station. All were talking at once, indeed, when the rear door opened and in came the conductor, escorting the shivering Isadore.

"Does this—this *tyke* belong in here?" demanded the man of brass buttons, with much emphasis.

They welcomed him loudly. The conductor shook his head. The flagman on the end of the train had helped the boy aboard the last car as the train started to move.

"Keep him here!" commanded the conductor. "And I've a mind to have both doors of the car locked until we reach Logwood. Don't let me hear anything more from you boys and girls on this journey."

He went away laughing, however, and bye and bye they

quieted down. Madge insisted upon making some hot composition, very strong, and dosing Isadore with it. The drink probably warded off a cold. Izzy admitted to Bobbins that a sister wasn't so bad to "have around" after all.

While they slept, the car was shunted to the sidetrack at Logwood and the western-bound train went hooting away through the forest. It was still snowing heavily, there were not many trains passing through the Logwood yard, and no switching during the early part of the day. The snow smothered other sounds.

Therefore, the party that had come to the lake for a vacation was not astir until late. It was hunger that roused them to the realities of life in the end. They had to dress and go to the one hotel of which the settlement boasted for breakfast.

"Can't cross to the island on the ice, they say," Ralph Tingley ran in to tell his mother. "Weight of the snow has broken it up. One of the men says he'll get a punt and pole us over to Cliff Island if the snow stops so that he can see his way."

"My! won't that be fun!" gasped Ann Hicks, who had overheard him.

She had begun to enjoy herself the minute she felt that they were in rough country. Some of the girls wished they hadn't come. Ruth and Helen were already outside, snowballing with the boys.

When Mrs. Tingley descended the car steps, ready to go to breakfast, her other son appeared—a second Mercury.

"Mother, Mr. Preston is here. Says he'd like to see you."

Mr. Preston was the foreman to whom Jerry Sheming had

Alice B. Emerson

been sent for a job. Ruth, who overheard, remembered the man's name. Then she saw a man dressed in Canadian knit cap, tall boots, and mackinaw, and carrying a huge umbrella, with which he hurried forward to hold protectingly over Mrs. Tingley's head.

"Glad to see you, ma'am," said the foreman. Ruth was passing them on her way to the hotel when she heard something that stayed her progress. "Sorry to trouble you. Mr. Tingley ain't coming up to-day?"

"Not until Christmas morning," replied the lady. "He cannot get away before."

"Well, I'll have to discharge that Jerry Sheming. Too bad, too. He's a worker, and well able to guide the boys and girls around the island—knows it like a book."

"Why let him go, then?" asked the lady.

"Blent says he's dishonest. An' I seen him snooping around rather funny, myself. Guess I'll have to fire him, Mis' Tingley."

CHAPTER XII

RUFUS BLENT'S LITTLE WAYS

The crowd waded through the soft snow to the inn. It was a small place, patronized mainly by fishermen and hunters in the season. It was plain, from the breakfast they served to the Tingley party, that if the unexpected guests had to remain long, they would be starved to death.

"And all the 'big eats' over on the Island," wailed Heavy. "I could swim there, I believe."

"I am afraid I could not allow you to do that," said Mrs. Tingley, shaking her head. "It would be too absurd. We'd better take the train home again."

"Never!" chorused Belle and her brothers. "We must get to Cliff Island in some way—by hook or by crook," added the girl, who had set her heart upon this outing.

Ruth was rather serious this morning. She waited for a chance to speak with Mrs. Tingley alone, and when it came, she blurted out what she wished to say:

"Oh, Mrs. Tingley! I couldn't help hearing what that man said to you. Must he discharge Jerry because Rufus Blent

Alice B. Emerson

says so?"

"Why, my dear! Oh! I remember. You were the girl who befriended the boy in the first place?"

"Yes, I did, Mrs. Tingley. And I hope you won't let your foreman turn him off for nothing—"

"Oh! I can't interfere. It is my husband's business, of course."

"But let me tell you!" urged Ruth, and then she related all she knew about Jerry Sheming, and all about the story of the old hunter who had lived so many years on Cliff Island.

"Mr. Tingley had a good deal of trouble over that squatter," said Belle's mother, slowly. "He was crazy."

"That might be. But Jerry isn't crazy."

"But they made some claim to owning a part of the island."

"And after the old man had lived there for fifty years, perhaps he thought he had a right to it."

"Why, my child, that sounds reasonable. But of course he didn't."

"Just the same," said Ruth, "he maybe had the box of money and papers hidden on the island, as he said. That is what Jerry has been looking for. And I wager that man Blent is afraid he will find it."

"How romantic!" laughed Mrs. Tingley.

"But, do wait till Mr. Tingley comes and let him decide," begged Ruth.

"Surely. And I will tell Mr. Preston to refuse any of Blent's demands. He is a queer old fellow, I know. And, come to think of it, he told us he wanted to make some investigations regarding the caves at the west end of the island. He wouldn't sell us the place without reserving in the deed the rights to all mineral deposits and to treasure trove."

"What's 'treasure trove,' Mrs. Tingley?" asked Ruth, quickly.

"Why—that would mean anything valuable found upon the land which is not naturally a part of it."

"Like a box of money, or papers?"

"Yes! I see. I declare, child, maybe the boy, Jerry, has told you the truth!"

"I am sure he has. He seemed like a perfectly honest boy," declared Ruth, anxiously.

"I will see Mr. Preston again," spoke Mrs. Tingley, decisively.

The storm continued through the forenoon. But the boys and girls waiting for transportation to Cliff Island had plenty of fun.

Behind the inn was an open field, and there they built a fort, the party being divided into opposing armies. Tom Cameron led one and Ann Hicks was chosen to head the other. Mercy could look at them from the windows, and urge the girls on in the fray.

The boys might throw straighter, but numbers told. The girls could divide and attack the boy defenders of the fortress on both flanks. They came in rosy and breathless at noon—to sit

Alice B. Emerson

down to a most heart-breaking luncheon.

"Such an expanse of table and so little on it I never saw before," grumbled Heavy, in a glum aside. "How long do you suppose we would exist on these rations?"

"We're not dead yet," said Ruth, cheerfully, "so you needn't become a 'gloom.'"

"Jen ought to live on past meals—like a camel existing on its hump," declared Madge.

"I'm no camel," retorted the plump one, instantly. "And a meal to me—after it has been digested—is nothing more than a beautiful dream; and you can bet that I never gained my avoirdupois by dreaming!"

Mrs. Tingley beckoned to Ruth after dinner. Together they went into the general room, where there was a huge fire of logs. Mr. Preston, the foreman, was there.

"I have been making inquiries," the lady explained to Ruth, "and I find that this Rufus Blent has not a very enviable reputation. At least, he is considered, locally, a sharper."

"Is this the girl who is interested in Jerry?" asked the foreman. "Well! he ought to be all right if she sticks up for him."

"I believe his story is true," Ruth said, shaking her head.

"And if that's so, then the boss hasn't got a clear title to Cliff Island—eh?" returned the big foreman, smiling at her quizzically.

"That isn't Mr. Tingley s fault," cried Ruth, quickly.

"He'd be the one to suffer, however, if it should be proved that old Pete Tilton had any vested right in the island," said Preston. "You can bet Blent is sharp enough to have covered his tracks if he has done anything foxy. He was never caught yet in any legal tangle."

"Oh, I hope Mr. Tingley won't have trouble up here," declared Mrs. Tingley, quite disturbed.

Ruth felt rather embarrassed. As much as she was interested in Jerry Sheming, she did not like to think she was stirring up trouble for her school-mate's father. Just then the outer door of the inn opened and a man entered, stamping the snow from his boots upon the wire mat.

"S-s-t!" said Preston, his eyes twinkling. "Here's Rufus Blent himself."

It seemed that Mrs. Tingley had never seen the real estate man and she was quite as much interested as Ruth in making his acquaintance. They both eyed him with growing disapproval as the old man finished freeing his feet of the clinging snow and then charged at Preston from across the big room.

"I say! I say, you, Preston!" he snarled. "Have you done what I tol' you? Have you got that Jerry Sheming off the island? He'd never oughter been let to git on there ag'in. I've been away, or I'd heard of it before. Is he off?"

"Not yet," replied Preston, smiling secretly.

"I wanter know why not? I won't have him snoopin' around there. It was understood when I sold Tingley that island that I reserved sartain rights—"

Alice B. Emerson

"This here is Mis' Tingley," interposed Preston, turning the old man's attention to the lady.

He was a brown, wrinkled old man, with sparse pepper-and-salt whiskers and a parrot-like nose. "Sharper" was written all over his hatchet features; but probably his provincialism and lack of book education had kept him from being a very dangerous villain.

"I wanter know!" exclaimed Rufus. "So you're Tingley's lady? Wal! do you take charge here?"

"Oh, no," laughed Mrs. Tingley. "My husband will be up here Christmas morning."

"Goin' to have Preston send that boy back to the mainland?"

"Oh, no, I shall not interfere. Mr. Tingley will attend to it when he comes. I think that would be best."

"Nothin' of the kind!" cried Blent, his little eyes snapping. "That boy's got no business over there—snooping round."

"What are you afraid of, Rufus? What do you think he'll find?" queried Preston, who was evidently not above aggravating the old fellow.

"Never you mind! Never you mind!" croaked Blent. "If you folks won't discharge him and put him off the island, I'll do it, myself."

"How can you, Mr. Blent?" asked Mrs. Tingley, feeling some disposition to cross swords with him.

"Never you mind. I'll do it. Goin' back to-day, of course, Preston; ain't you?"

"I'm hoping to get this crowd of young folk—and Mrs. Tingley—across to the island. And I think the snow is going to stop soon."

"I'll go with you," declared Blent, promptly. "Don't you go till I see you again, Preston. I gotter ketch 'Squire Keller fust."

He hurried out of the inn. Mrs. Tingley and Ruth looked at the foreman questioningly. The girl cried:

"Oh! what will he do?"

"He's going to get a warrant for the boy," answered Preston, scowling.

"How can he? What has Jerry done?"

"That don't make no difference," said the woodsman. "Old Rufus just about runs the politics of this town. Keller will do what he says. Rufus will get the boy off the island by foul means if he can't by fair."

Alice B. Emerson

CHAPTER XIII

FIGHTING FIRE WITH FIRE

Ruth felt her heart swell in anger against Rufus Blent, the Logwood real estate man. If she had not been determined before to aid Jerry Sheming in every way possible, she was now.

If there was a box of money and papers hidden on Cliff Island, once belonging to Pete Tilton, the old hunter, Ruth desired to keep Blent from finding it.

She believed Jerry's story—about the treasure box and all. Rufus Blent's actions now seemed to prove the existence of such a box. He wanted to find it. But if the money and papers in the box had belonged to old Pete Tilton, surely Jerry, as his single living relative, should have the best right to the "treasure trove."

How to thwart Blent was the question disturbing Ruth Fielding's mind. Of course, nobody but Jerry had as strong a desire as she to outwit the old real estate man. The other girls and boys—even Mrs. Tingley—would not feel as Ruth did about it. She knew that well enough.

If anything was to be done to save Jerry from being arrested on a false charge and dragged from Cliff Island by Blent, *she* must bring it about. Ruth watched the last flakes of the snow falling with a very serious feeling.

The other young folk were delighted with the breaking of the weather. Now they could observe Logwood better, and its surroundings. The roughly built "shanty-town" was dropped down on the edge of the lake, in a clearing. Much of the stumpage around the place was still raw. The only roads were timber roads and they were now knee-deep in fresh snow.

There was a dock with a good-sized steamer tied up at it, but there was too much ice for it to be got out into the lake. The railroad came out of the woods on one side and disappeared into just as thick a forest on the other.

The interest of the young people, however, lay in the bit of land that loomed up some five miles away. Cliff Island contained several hundred acres of forest and meadow—all now covered with glittering white.

At the nearer end was the new hunting lodge of the Tingleys, with the neighboring outbuildings. At the far end the island rose to a rugged promontory perhaps a hundred and fifty feet high, with a single tall pine tree at the apex.

That western end of the island seemed to be built of huge boulders for the most part. Here and there the rocks were so steep that the snow did not cling to them, and they looked black and raw against the background of dazzling white.

The face of the real cliff—because of which the island had received its name—was scarcely visible from Logwood. Jerry had told Ruth it was a very wild and desolate place, and the girl of the Red Hill could easily believe it.

The crowd had left the inn as soon as the clouds began to break and a ray or two of sunshine shone forth. Two ox teams were breaking the paths through the town. The boys and girls went down to the dock, singing and shouting. Mrs. Tingley and the foreman came behind.

Three other men were making ready a huge punt in which the entire party might be transported to the island. Later the punt would return for the extra baggage.

This vehicle for water-travel was a shallow, skiff-like boat, almost as broad as it was long, and with a square bow and stern. There was a place for a short mast to be stepped, but, with the lake covered with drifting ice cakes, it was judged safer to depend upon huge sweeps for motive power.

With these sweeps, not only could the punt be urged forward at a speed of perhaps two miles an hour, but the ice-cakes could be pushed aside and a channel opened through the drifting mass for the passage of the awkward boat.

Mr. Preston had explained all this to Mrs. Tingley, who was used to neither the woods nor the lake, and she had agreed that this means of transportation to Cliff Island was sufficiently safe, though extraordinary.

"Let's pile in and make a start," urged Ralph Tingley, eagerly. "Why! we won't get there by dark if we don't hurry."

"And goodness knows we need to get somewhere to eat before long," cried Jennie Stone. "I am willing to help propel the boat myself, if they'll show me how."

"You might get out and swim, and drag us behind you, Heavy," suggested one of the girls. "You're so anxious to get over to the island."

They all were desirous of gaining their destination—there could be no doubt of that. As they were getting aboard, however, there came a hail from up the main street of Logwood.

"Hi, yi! Don't you folks go without me! Hi, Preston!"

"Here comes that Blent man," said Mrs. Tingley, with some disgust. "I suppose we must take him?"

"Well, I wouldn't advise ye to turn him down, Mis' Tingley," urged the foreman. "No use making him your enemy. I tell you he's got a big political pull in these parts."

"Is there room for him?"

"Yes. And for the fellow with him. That's Lem Daggett, the constable. Oh, Rufe is going over with all the legal right on his side. He'll bring Jerry back here and shut him up for a few days, I suppose."

"But on what charge?" Mrs. Tingley asked, in some distress.

"That won't matter. Some trumped-up charge. Easy enough to do it when you have a feller like 'Squire Keller to deal with. Oh," said Preston, shaking his head, "Rufe Blent knows what he's about, you may believe!"

"Who's the old gee-gee with the whiskers?" asked the disrespectful Isadore, when the real estate man came down to the dock, with the constable slouching behind him.

"Hurry up, Grandpop!" shouted one of the Tingley boys. "This expedition is about to start."

Blent scowled at the hilarious crowd. It was plain to be seen that any supply of milk of human kindness he may have had was long since soured.

Ruth caught Tom Cameron's eye and nodded to him. Helen's twin was a very good friend of the girl from the Red Mill and he quickly grasped her wish to speak with him alone.

In a minute he maneuvered so as to get into the stern with his sister's chum, and there Ruth whispered to him her fears and desires regarding Blent and Jerry Sheming.

"Say! we ought to help that fellow. See what he did for Jane Ann," said Tom. "And that old fellow looks so sour he sets my teeth on edge, anyway."

"He is going to do a very mean thing," declared Ruth, decidedly. "Jerry has done nothing wrong, I am sure."

"We must beat the old fellow."

"But how, Tom? They say he is all-powerful here at Logwood."

"Let me think. I'll be back again," replied Tom, as the boys called him to come up front.

The punt was already under way. Preston and his three men worked the craft out slowly into the drifting ice. The grinding of the cakes against the sides of the boat did not frighten any of the passengers—unless perhaps Mrs. Tingley herself. She felt responsible for the safety of this whole party of her daughter's school friends.

The wind was not strong and the drift of the broken ice was slow. Therefore there was really no danger to be apprehended. The punt was worked along its course with considerable ease.

The boys had to take their turns at the sweeps; but Tom found time to slip back to Ruth before they were half-way across to the island.

"Too bad the old fellow doesn't fall overboard," he growled in Ruth's ear. "Isn't he a snarly old customer?"

"But I suppose the constable has the warrant," Ruth returned, smiling. "So Mr. Blent's elimination from the scene would not help Jerry much."

"I tell you what—you've got to fight fire with fire," observed Tom, after a moment of deep reflection.

"Well? What meanest thou, Sir Oracle?"

"Why, they haven't any business to arrest Jerry."

"Agreed."

"Then let's tip him off so that he can run."

"Where will he run to?" demanded Ruth, eagerly.

"Say! that's a big island. And I bet he knows his way all over it."

"Oh! the caves!" exclaimed Ruth.

"What's that?"

"He told me there were caves in it. He can hide in one. And we can get food to him. Great, Tom—great!"

"Sure it's great. When your Uncle Dudley—"

　　　　Alice B. Emerson

"But how are we going to warn Jerry to run before this constable catches him?" interposed Ruth, with less confidence.

"How? You leave that to me," Tom returned, mysteriously.

CHAPTER XIV

THE HUE AND CRY

Ruth and Tom Cameron had no further opportunity of speaking together until the punt came very close to the island. Here the current ran more swiftly and the ice-blocks seemed to have been cleared away.

There was a new stone dock, and up the slight rise from it, about a hundred yards back from the shore, was the heavily-framed lodge. It consisted of two stories, the upper one extending over the lower. Big beams crossed at the corners of this upper story and the outer walls were of roughly hewn logs. The great veranda was arranged for screening, in the summer, but now the west side was enclosed with glass. It was an expensive and comfortable looking camp.

There were several men on the dock as the punt came in, but Jerry Sheming was not in sight. Tom had, from time to time, been seen whispering with the boys. They all now gathered in the bow of the slowly moving punt, ready to leap ashore the moment she bumped into the dock.

"Do be careful, boys," begged Mrs. Tingley. "Don't fall into the water, or get hurt. I certainly shall be glad when Mr. Tingley comes up for Christmas and takes all this responsibility off my hands."

"Don't have any fear for us, Mrs. Tingley, I beg," said Tom. "We're only going to scramble ashore, and the first fellow who reaches the house is the best man. Now, fellows!"

The punt bumped. Such a scrambling as there was! Ann Hicks showed her suppleness by being one of the first to land and beating some of the boys; but she did not run with them.

"They might have stayed and helped us girls—and Mrs. Tingley—to land," complained Helen. "I don't see what Tom was thinking of."

But all of a sudden Ruth had an idea that she understood Tom's lack of gallantry. Jerry Sheming, not being at the dock to meet the newcomers, must be at the house. The boys, it proved later, had agreed to help "tip" Jerry. The first fellow to see him was to tell him of the approach of Blent and the constable.

Therefore, when Rufus Blent and Lem Daggett reached the lodge, nobody seemed to know anything about Jerry. Tom winked knowingly at Ruth.

"I tell ye, Preston, I gotter take that boy back to Logwood with me," shouted Blent, who seemed greatly excited. "Where are you hidin' the rascal?"

"You know very well I came over with you in the boat and walked up here with you, Blent," growled the foreman, in some anger. "How could I hide him?"

"But the cook, nor nobody, knows what's become of him. He was here peelin' 'taters for supper, cookie says, jest b'fore we landed. Now he's sloped."

"He saw you comin', it's likely," rejoined Preston. "He suspected what you was after."

"Well, I'm goin' to leave Daggett. And, Lem!"

"Yes, sir?" said that slouching person.

"You got to get him. Now mind that. The boy's to 'pear in 'Squire Keller's court to-morrow—or something will happen," threatened the real estate man.

"And if he don't appear, what then?" drawled Preston, who was more amused by the old man than afraid of him.

"You'd better not interfere with the course of the law, Preston," declared Blent, shaking his head.

"You bet I won't. Especially the brand of law that's handed a feller by your man, Keller. But I don't know nothing about the boy nor where he's gone. I don't wanter know, either.

"And none of they rest o' you wanter harbor that thief," snarled Blent, viciously, looking around at the gaping hired men and the boys who had come to visit Cliff Island. "The law's got a long arm. 'Member that!"

"Will we be breaking the law if we don't report this poor fellow to the constable here, if we see him?" asked Tom Cameron, boldly.

"You bet you will. And I'll see that you're punished if ye harbor or help the rascal. Don't think because Tingley's a rich man, and your fathers have probably more money than is good for them, that you will escape," said Blent.

"I don't believe he's so powerful as he makes out to be,"

grumbled Tom, later, to Ruth. "*I* was the one who caught Jerry and whispered for him to get out. I didn't have to say much to him. He was wise about Blent."

"Where did he go?" asked the eager Ruth, quickly.

"I don't know. I didn't want to know—and you don't, either. '

"But suppose something happens to him?" objected the girl, fearfully.

"Why, he knows all about this island. You said so yourself. I just told him we'd get some grub to him to-morrow."

"How?"

"Told him we'd leave it at the foot of that tall pine at the far end of the island. Then he slipped out of the kitchen and disappeared."

But Blent was a crafty old party and did not easily give up the pursuit of the young fellow he had come to the island to nab. The coat of fresh snow over everything made tracking the fugitive an easy task.

After a few minutes of sputtering anger, the real estate man organized a pursuit of Jerry. He made sure that the forest youth had run out of the kitchen at about the time the visitors came up from the dock.

"He ain't got a long start," said Blent to his satellite, the constable. "Let's see if he didn't leave tracks."

He had. There was still an hour of daylight, although the winter evening was closing in rapidly. Jerry had left by the back door of the lodge and had gone straight across the yard, through the unbroken snow, to the bunkhouse used by the male help.

There he had stopped for his rifle and shotgun, and ammunition. Indeed, he had taken everything that belonged to him, and, loaded down with this loot, had gone right up the hill, keeping in the scrub so as to be hidden from the big house, and had so passed over the rising ground toward the middle of the island.

"The track is plain enough," Blent said. "Ain't ye got a dog, Preston? We could foller him all night."

"Not with our dogs," declared the foreman.

"Why not?"

"Don't think the boss would like it. We don't keep dogs to hunt men with."

"You better take care how you try to block the law," threatened the old man. "That boy's goin' to be caught."

"Not with these dogs," grunted Preston. "You can put *that* in your pipe and smoke it."

Blent and the constable went off over the ridge. Ruth was so much interested that she stole out to follow them, and Ann Hicks overtook her before she had gotten far up the track.

"Ruth Fielding! whatever are you doing?" demanded the girl from the Montana ranch. "Don't you know it will soon be night? Mrs. Tingley says for you to come back."

"Do you suppose those horrid men will find Jerry?"

Alice B. Emerson

"No, I don't," replied Ann, shortly. "And if they do—"

"Oh! you're not as interested in him as I am," sighed Ruth. "I am sure he is honest and that Mr. Blent is telling lies about him. I—I want to see that they don't abuse him if they catch him."

"Abuse him! And he a backwoods boy, with two guns?" snorted Ann. "Why, he wouldn't even let them arrest him, I don't suppose. *I* wouldn't if I were Jerry."

"But that would be dreadful," sighed Ruth. "Let's go a little farther, Ann."

Dusk was falling, however, and when they got down the far side of the ridge they came to a swift, open water-course. Blent and the constable were evidently "stumped." Blent was snarling at their ill-luck.

"He's took to the water—that's all *I* know," drawled Lem Daggett, the constable. "Ye see, there ain't a mark in the snow on 'tother side."

"Him wadin' in that ice-cold stream in mid-winter," grunted Blent. "Ain't he a scoundrel?"

"Can't do nothin' more to-night," announced the constable, who didn't like the job any too well, it was evident. "And dorgs wouldn't do us no good."

"Ha! ye know what ye gotter do," threatened Blent. "I'm goin' back to town when the punt goes this evenin'. But you stay here, an' you git the hue an' cry out after him to-morrer bright and early.

"I don't want him rummagin' around this island at all. You

understand? Not at all! It's up to you to git him, Lem Daggett."

Daggett grunted and followed his master back to the lodge. The girls went on before and Ruth was delighted that, for a time, at least, Jerry was to have his freedom.

"If it froze over solid in the night he could get to the mainland from the other end of the island, and then they'd never find him," she confided to Tom.

But when morning came the surface of the lake was still a mass of loose and shifting ice. Lem demanded of Mrs. Tingley the help of all the men at the camp, and they started right away after breakfast to "comb" the island in a thorough manner.

There wasn't a trace near the running stream to show in which direction the fugitive had gone. Had Jerry gone up stream he could have reached the very heart of the rough end of the island without leaving the water-trail.

A party of the boys, with Ruth, Helen, and Ann Hicks, stole out of the lodge after the main searching party, and struck off for the high point where the lone pine tree grew.

"I'd hate to think we'd draw that constable over there and help him to catch Jerry," said Bobbins.

"We won't," Tom replied. "We are just going to leave the tin box of grub for him. He probably won't come out of hiding and try to get the food until this foolish constable has given up the chase. And I put the food in the tin box so that no prowling animal would get it instead of Jerry."

It was hard traveling in the snow, for the party of young folk had not thought to obtain snowshoes. "We'll string some when we go back," Tom promised. "I know there are some frames all ready."

"But no more such tobogganing as we had last winter up at Snow Camp," declared Busy Izzy, with deep feeling. "Remember the spill I had with Ruth and that Heavy girl? Gee! that was some spill."

"The land here Is too rough for good sliding," said Tom. "But I wish the lake would freeze hard again. Ralph says there are a couple of good scooters, and we all have our skates."

"And the fishing!" exclaimed Helen, eagerly. "I *do* so want to fish through the ice again."

"Oh! we're bound to have a bully good time," declared Bobbins. "But we'll do this Jerry Sheming a good turn, too, if we can."

CHAPTER XV

OVER THE PRECIPICE

Under the soft snow that had fallen the day before was a hard-packed layer that had come earlier in the season and made a firm footing for the explorers. Ruth and her chum, with Ann Hicks, were quite as good walkers as the boys. At any rate, the three girls determined not to be at the end of the procession.

The constable and his unwilling helpers (for none of the men about the Tingley camp cared to see Jerry Sheming in trouble) were hunting the banks of the stream higher up for traces of the trail the boy had taken when he ran away from Rufus Blent the previous afternoon.

Therefore the girls and boys who had started for the rendezvous at the lone pine, were able to put the wooded ridge between them and the constable's party, and so make their way unobserved toward the western end of Cliff Island.

"They may come back and follow us," growled Tom. "But they'll be some way behind, and we'll hurry. I have a note in this tin box warning Jerry what he must look out for. As long as that Lem Daggett is on the island, I suppose he will be in danger of arrest."

Alice B. Emerson

"It is just as mean as it can be!" gasped Helen, plodding on.

"The boys wouldn't leave much o' that constable if they caught him playin' tag for such a man as Blent, at Bullhide." Ann Hicks declared, with warmth.

"This Blent," said Bobbins, seriously, "seems to have everybody about Logwood buffaloed. What do you suppose your father will say to the constable taking the men with him this morning to hunt Jerry down?"

This question he put to Ralph Tingley and the latter flushed angrily.

"You wait!" he exclaimed. "Father will be angry, I bet. I told mother not to let the men have anything to do with the hunt, but you know how women are. She was afraid. She said that if Blent and the constable were within their legal rights—"

"All bosh!" snapped Isadore Phelps.

"I do not think Mrs. Tingley would have let them go with Daggett if she'd had the least idea they would be able to find Jerry," observed Helen, sagely.

"And they won't," put in Ruth, with assurance. "I know he can hide away on this island like a fox in a burrow."

"But he'll find it mighty cold sleeping out, this weather," remarked Bobbins.

"He sure will!" agreed Tom.

The party went ahead as rapidly as possible, but even the stronger of the boys found it hard to climb the steeper ascents through the deep snow.

"Crackey!" exclaimed Isadore. "I know I'm slipping back two steps to every one I get ahead."

"Nonsense, Izzy," returned Helen. "For if you did *that*, you had better turn around and travel the other way; then you'd back up the hill!"

They had to wait and rest every few yards. The rocks were so huge that they often had to go out of the way for some distance to get around them. Although it could not be more than five miles, as the crow flies, from the lodge to the lone pine, in two hours they still had the hardest part of the journey before them.

"I had no idea we should be so long at it," Tom confessed.

"It's lucky Heavy didn't come with us," chuckled Helen.

"Why?"

"She would have been starved to death before this, and the idea of going the rest of the distance before turning back for home and luncheon would have destroyed her reason, I am sure."

"Then," said Ruth, amused by this extravagant language, "poor Heavy would have been first dead and then crazy! Consider an insane corpse!"

They came out at last upon the foot of the last ascent. The eminence seemed to be a smooth, cone-shaped hill. On it grew a number of trees, but the enormous old pine, lightning-riven and dead at the top, stood much taller than any of the other trees.

Here and there they caught glimpses of chasms and steep

Alice B. Emerson

ravines that seemed to split the rocky island to the edge of the water. When the snow did not cover the ground there might be paths to follow, but at this time the young explorers had to use their judgment in climbing the heights as best they might.

The boys had to help the girls up the steeper places, with all their independence, and even Ann admitted that their male comrades were "rather handy to have about."

The old pine tree sprang out of a little hollow in the hill. Behind it was the peak of the island, and from this highest spot the party obtained an unobstructed view of the whole western end of Tallahaska.

"It's one big old lake," sighed Isadore Phelps. "If it would only just freeze over, boys, and give us a chance to try out the iceboats!"

"If it keeps on being as cold as it was this morning, and the wind dies down, there'll be all the ice you want to see to-morrow," declared Ralph Tingley. "Goodness! let's get down from this exposed place. I'm 'most frozen."

"Shall we stop and make a fire here, girls, and warm up before we return?" asked Tom Cameron.

"And draw that constable right to this place where you want to leave Jerry's tin box?" cried his sister. "No, indeed!"

"We'd better keep moving, anyway," Ruth urged. "Less danger of frost-bite. The wind *is* keen."

Tom had already placed the box of food in a sheltered spot. "The meat will be frozen as solid as a rock, I s'pose," he grumbled. "I hope that poor fellow has some way of making a fire in his hide-out."

They began to retrace their steps. Instead of following exactly the same path they had used in climbing to the summit, Tom struck off at an angle, believing he saw an easier way.

His companions followed him in single file. Ruth happened to be the last of all to come down the smooth slope. The seven ahead of her managed to tramp quite a smooth track through the snow, and once or twice she slipped in stepping in their footprints.

"Look out back there, Ruthie!" called Tom, from the lead. "The snow must have got balled on your boots. Knock it off—"

His speech was halted by a startled cry from Ruth. She felt herself going and threw out both hands to say her sudden slide.

But there was nothing for her hands to seize save the unstable snow itself. She fell on her side, and shot out from the narrow track her companions had trod.

"Ruth!" shrieked Helen, in the wildest kind of dismay.

But the girl of the Red Mill was already out of reach. The drifting snow had curled out over the brink of the tall rock across the brow of which Tom had unwisely led the way. They had not realized they were so near the verge of the precipice.

Ruth's body was solid, and when she fell in the snow the undercrust broke like an eggshell. Amid a cloud of snow-dust she shot over the yawning edge of the chasm and disappeared.

Alice B. Emerson

Several square yards of the snow-drift had broken away. At their very feet fell the unexpected precipice. The boys and girls shrank back from the peril with terrified cries, clinging to each other.

"She is killed!" moaned Helen, and covered her face with her mittened hands.

"Ruth! Ruth!" called Tom, charging back toward the broken snow-drift.

But Bobbins caught and held him. "Don't make a fool of yourself, old man!" commanded the big fellow. "You can't help her by falling over the cliff yourself."

"Oh! how deep can that place be?" gasped Ralph Tingley.

"What will mother say?" cried his brother.

"Ruth! Ruth!" shouted Ann Hicks, and dropped on her knees to crawl to the edge.

"You'll be down there yourself, Ann!" exclaimed Helen, sobbing.

"A couple of you useless boys grab me by the ankles," commanded the western girl. "Come! take a good hold. Now let me see—"

She hung half over the verge of the rock. The fall was sheer for fifty feet at least. It was a narrow cut in the hill, with apparently unscalable sides and open only toward the lake.

"I—I don't see a thing,' panted the girl.

"Shout again," urged Helen.

"Let's all shout together!" cried Isadore. "Now!"

They raised their voices in a long, lingering yell. Again and again they repeated it. They thought nothing now of the possibility of attracting the constable and his companions to the scene.

Meanwhile nothing but the echoes replied to their hail. Down there in the chasm Ann Hicks saw no sign of the lost girl. The bottom of the place seemed heaped high with snow.

"She plunged right into the drift, and perhaps she's smothered down there," gasped Ann. "Oh! what shall we do?"

"If it's a deep drift Ruth may not be hurt at all," cried Tom. "Do let me look, Ann. That's a good girl."

The western girl was drawn back and the boy took her place. Bobbins and Ralph Tingley let Tom slide farther over the verge of the precipice than they had Ann.

"She went down feet first," panted Tom. "There isn't an obstruction she could have hit. She must have dropped right into the snowbank in the bottom—Ruth! Ruth Fielding!"

But even his sharp eyes could discover no mark in the snow. Nothing of the lost girl appeared above the drift at the foot of this sheer cliff. She might have been smothered under the snow, as Ann suggested. And yet, that scarcely seemed probable.

Surely the fall into the soft drift could not have injured Ruth fatally. She must have had strength enough to struggle to the surface of the snow.

Her disappearance was a most mysterious thing. When Tom

Alice B. Emerson

crept back from the brink of the precipice and stood on his feet again, they all stared at one another in growing wonder.

"What could have happened to her down there?" groaned Helen, her own amazement stifling her sobs.

CHAPTER XVI

HIDE AND SEEK

Ruth had fallen with but a single shriek. From top to bottom of the precipice had been such a swift descent that she could not cry out a second time. And the great bank of snow into which she had plunged did—as Ann suggested—smother her.

The shock of dropping fifty feet through the air, and landing without experiencing anything more dangerous than a greatly accelerated heart-action was enough, of itself, to make the girl of the Red Mill dumb for the moment.

She heard faintly the frightened cries of her companions, and she struggled to get to the surface of the great, soft heap of snow that had saved her from instant death.

Then she heard a voice pronounce her name, and a hand was thrust into the snow bank and seized her shoulder.

"Ruth Fielding! Miss Ruth! That come nigh to being your last jump, that did!"

"Jerry Sheming!" gasped the girl, as he drew her out of the snow.

Alice B. Emerson

"In here—quick! Are they after me?"

Ruth shook the snow from her eyes. She was like a half-drowned person suddenly coming to the surface.

"Where—where are we?" she whispered.

"All right! This is one of my hide-outs. Is that old Blent up yonder?"

"Oh, Jerry! he's not on the island to-day. He's left the constable—"

"Lem Daggett?"

"Yes. They are searching for you. But I was with Tom and Helen and the others. We brought you some food—"

He led her along a narrow shelf, which had been swept quite free of snow. Now a hollow in the rock-wall opened before them, and there a little fire of sticks burned, an old buffalo robe lay nearby, and there were other evidences of the fugitive's camp.

Ruth was shaking now, but not from the cold. The shock of her fall had begun to awaken the nervous terror which is the afterclap of such an adventure. So near she had been to death!

"You are sick, Miss Ruth?" exclaimed Jerry.

"Oh, no! Oh, no!" repeated the girl of the Red Mill. "But so—so frightened."

"Nothin' to be frightened over now," he returned, smiling broadly. "But you *did* miss it close. If that pile of snow hadn't sifted down there yesterday—"

"I know!" burst out Ruth. "It was providential."

"You girls and boys want to be careful climbing around these rocks," said Jerry Sheming, gravely.

At that moment the chorus of shouts from above reached their ears. Ruth turned about and her lips opened. She would have replied, but the backwoods boy leaped across the fire and seized her arm.

"Don't make a sound!" he exclaimed.

"Oh! Jerry—"

"If that constable hears—"

"He isn't with us, I tell you," said Ruth.

"But wait. He might hear. I don't want him to find this place," spoke the boy, eagerly. "He may be within hearing."

"No. I think not," Ruth explained. Then she told Jerry of the morning's hunt for him and the course followed by both parties. He shook his head for a moment, and then ran to a shelf at the other side of the little cavern.

"I'll communicate with your friends. I'll make them understand. But we mustn't shout. Lem Daggett may be within hearing."

"But I can't stay with you here, Jerry," objected the girl.

"Of course you can't, Miss. I will get you out—another way. You'll see. But we'll explain to your friends above and they

Alice B. Emerson

will stop yelling then. If they keep on that way they'll draw Lem Daggett here, if he isn't already snooping around."

Meanwhile Jerry had found a scrap of paper and a pencil. He hurriedly wrote a few lines upon the paper. Then he produced a heavy bow and a long arrow. The message he tied around the shank of the arrow.

"Oh! can you shoot with that?" cried Ruth, much interested.

"Reckon so," grinned Jerry. "Uncle Pete wouldn't give me much powder and shot when I was a kid. And finally I could bring home a bigger bag of wild turkeys than he could, and all I had to get 'em with was this bow'n'arrer."

He strung the bow, and Ruth saw that it took all his strength to do it. The boys and girls were still shouting for her in a desultory fashion. Jerry laid his finger on his lips, nodded at his visitor, and stepped swiftly out of sight along the cleared shelf of rock.

Ruth left the fire to peer after him. She saw him bend the bow and saw the swift flight of the arrow as it shot out of the chasm and curved out of sight beyond the broken edge of the snow-wreath which masked the summit of the cliff.

She heard the clamor of her friends' voices as they saw the arrow shoot over their heads. Then they were silent.

Jerry ran back to her and unstrung the bow, putting it away in its niche. But from the same place he produced a blue-barrelled rifle.

"I know you won't tell Blent, or any of them, how to reach me, Miss Ruth," he said, looking at her with a smile.

"I guess not!" exclaimed the girl.

"I am going to show you the way out—to the other end. I wish you were wearing rubber boots like me."

"Why?"

"So you could wade in the stream when we come to it. That's how I threw them off the track," explained Jerry, laughing. "Why, I know this old island better than Uncle Pete himself knowed it."

"And yet you haven't found the box you say your uncle hid?" asked Ruth, curiously.

"No. I never knowed anything about it until Blent came to drive us off and swore that Uncle Pete had never had nothin' but 'squatter rights.' But I'm not sure that I couldn't find that place where Uncle Pete hid his treasure box—if I had time to hunt for it," added Jerry, gravely.

"That's what Mr. Blent is afraid of," declared Ruth, with conviction. "That's why he is afraid of your being here on the island."

"You bet it is, Miss."

"And we boys and girls will do everything we can to help you, Jerry," Ruth assured him, warmly. "If you think you can find the place where your uncle hid his papers—"

"But suppose I find them and the papers show that this Mr. Tingley hasn't a clear title to the island?" demanded the backwoods boy, looking at the girl of the Red Mill sharply.

"Why should *that* make a difference?" asked Ruth, coolly.

"Well—you know how some of these rich folks be," returned the boy, dropping his gaze. "When it comes to hittin' their pocketbooks—"

"That has nothing to do with it. Right is right."

"Uh-huh!" grunted Jerry. "But sometimes they don't want to lose money any quicker than a poor man. If he's paid for the island—"

"I don't see how he can lose," declared Ruth, quickly. "If Blent has claimed a title that cannot be proved, Blent will have to lose."

"I bet Mr. Tingley didn't buy without having the title searched," observed Jerry. "Blent's covered his tracks. He'll declare he was within his rights, probably having bought Uncle Pete's share of the island through some dummy. You know, when deeds aren't recorded, it's mighty hard to establish them as valid. I know. I axed our town clerk. And he is one man that ain't under Blent's thumb."

"I don't believe Mr. Tingley is a man who would stand idle and see you cheated even if he lost money through defending you," said Ruth, firmly.

"Do you know him?"

"No. I have never met him," Ruth admitted. "But his wife is a very nice lady. And Belle and the boys—"

"Business is business," interrupted Jerry, shaking his head. "I don't want Tingley to know where I be—yet awhile, anyway."

"But may I talk with him about you?"

"Why—if you care enough to, Miss Ruth."

"Of course I do," cried the girl. "Didn't I tell you we all want to help you?" and she stamped her foot upon the warm rock. "We'll bring you food, too. We'll see that the constable doesn't get you."

"Well, it's mighty nice of you," admitted the suspicious young woodsman. "Now, come on. I'll take you through my hide-out to the creek. I told your friends you'd meet 'em there, and we want to get there by the time they arrive."

"Oh, Jerry! that's a long way off," cried Ruth.

"Not so very long by the way we'll travel," he returned, with a laugh.

And this proved to be true. Jerry lighted a battered oil lantern and with his rifle in the other hand led the way.

A narrow passage opened out of the back of this almost circular cave. Part of the time they traveled through a veritable tunnel. At other times Ruth saw the clear sky far above them as they passed along deep cuts in the hills.

The descent was continuous, but gradual. Such a path wild animals might have traveled in times past. Originally it was probably a water-course. The action of the water had eaten out the softer rock until almost a direct passage had been made from the bottom of the cliff where Ruth had fallen to the edge of the swift stream that ran through the middle of the island.

They came out behind a screen of thick brush through which Ruth could see the far bank of the brook, but through which nobody outside could see. Jerry set down the lantern, and

Alice B. Emerson

later leaned the rifle against the wall when he had made sure that nobody was in sight.

"I am going to carry you a ways, Miss Ruth," he said, "if you don't mind. You see, I must walk in the stream or they will find this entrance to my hide-out."

"But—can you carry me?"

"I bet you! If you only wore rubber boots I'd let you walk. Come on, please."

"Oh! I am not afraid," she told him, quietly, and allowed him to take her into his arms after he had stepped down into the shallow, swiftly lowing current.

"This water-trail confuses men and dogs completely," said Jerry, with a laugh. "That is—such men as Lem Daggett. If *I* was hunting a fellow who took to the stream, with the water so shallow, I'd find which way he went in a jiffy."

"How would you?" demanded Ruth, feeling perfectly secure in the strong arms of the young fellow.

"That's telling," chuckled Jerry. "Mebbe—some time—I'll tell you. I hoped I'd get the chance of showing you and your friends around this island. But I guess I won't."

"Perhaps you will. And if there is anything we can do to help you—"

"Just one thing you might do," remarked Jerry, finally setting her upright upon a flat rock on the side of the stream nearest the hunting camp, and some distance away from the secret entrance to his hide-out.

"Oh! what is that?" cried Ruth, eagerly.

"Find me a pickax, or a mattock, and put it right here on this rock. Do it at night, so no one will see you. Good bye, Miss!" he exclaimed, and hurried away.

In another minute he had disappeared behind the screen of bushes, and Ruth heard the glad shouts of her friends as they came over the ridge and saw her standing safe and sound beside the stream.

Alice B. Emerson

CHAPTER XVII

CHRISTMAS MORNING

"How under the sun did you get here, Ruth?" Helen shouted the moment she saw her chum.

"Did that Jerry Sheming bring you?" demanded Ann.

The other members of the party were quite as anxious to learn the particulars of her adventure, and when they had crossed on the stepping stones, they gathered about her eagerly.

Ruth would tell just so much and no more. She explained how she had fallen into the snow-drift at the foot of the cliff, how Jerry had heard her scream and pulled her out. But beyond that she only said he had left her here to wait their coming.

"You needn't be so mysterious, Miss!" ejaculated Helen, rather piqued.

"I guess she doesn't want to say anything about his hide-out that might lead to his being hunted out by Lem Daggett," observed the wise Tom. "But Jerry signed his name to the note he tied on the arrow."

"And we sure were surprised when we saw that arrow shoot up from the depths," said Isadore.

"What do you suppose mother will say?" cried one of the Tingley boys.

"Don't let's tell her," suggested Ruth, quickly. "There's no need. It will only add to her worries and she will be troubled enough by us as it is."

"But—"

"You see, I'm not a bit hurt," insisted Ruth. "And the less we talk about the matter the less likely we shall be to drop something that may lead to the discovery of Jerry Sheming's hiding place."

"Oh, well, if you put it that way," agreed Ralph. "I suppose mother will have all the trouble she wants. And maybe if she knew, she'd keep you girls away from this end of the island."

They tramped home to a late luncheon. It was so very cold that afternoon and evening that they were only too glad to remain in the house and "hug the fire."

The inclement weather drove Lem Daggett and the men indoors, too. The constable had to go back to Logwood without his prisoner, and he evidently feared the anger of Rufus Blent.

"I want to warn ye, Mis' Tingley," he said to the lady of the lodge, shaking his head, "that when Blent sets out ter do a thing, he does it. That boy's got to be found, and he's got to be kep' off this island."

"I will see what my husband says when he comes," replied

Alice B. Emerson

Mrs. Tingley, firmly. "I will not allow our men to chase the poor fellow further."

"You'd better ketch him and signal us at Logwood. Run up that flag on the pole outside. I'll know what you mean."

"Mr. Tingley will decide when he comes," was all the satisfaction the lady gave the constable.

After he had gone, Mrs. Tingley told Ruth she hoped no harm would come to the poor boy, "sleeping out in the cold alone."

"Oh, Mrs. Tingley! I know he has a warm, dry place to sleep, and plenty of firewood—heaps and heaps of it."

"You seem to know a good deal about him," the lady commented.

"Yes, I do," admitted Ruth, honestly. "More about him and where he is hiding than he would care to have me tell you."

So Mrs. Tingley did not catechise the girl further upon the subject of the fugitive.

Just because they were shut in was no reason why the house party on Cliff Island should not have an extraordinarily good time. They played games and had charades that evening. They had a candy pull, too, but unlike that famous one at Snow Camp the winter before, Busy Izzy Phelps did not get a chance to put the walnut shells into the taffy instead of the kernels.

The wind died down and it grew desperately cold during the night. The mercury soon left the zero point so far above that it threatened to be lost for the rest of the winter.

They awoke the next morning to find the island chained fast to the mainland by old Jack Frost's fetters. A sheet of new ice extended for some hundreds of yards all around Cliff Island. Farther out the ice was of rougher texture, but that near at hand was clear and black.

Out came the skates soon after breakfast, and everybody but Mercy went down to the lake. Later the boys made the lame girl and Mrs. Tingley come, too, and they arranged chairs in which the two non-skaters could be pushed over the smooth surface.

Hockey was the game for the afternoon, and two "sides" were chosen to oppose each other, one of the boys and another of the girls. Although Ann Hicks had never had a hockey stick in her hand before, she quickly got into the game, and they all had a very merry time.

The day before Ruth had not been able to find the implement that Jerry Sheming had spoken about, nor could she find a mattock, or pickax, on this second day. If she went to the toolshed and hunted for the thing herself she was afraid her quest would be observed by some of the men.

She located the place where the tools were kept, but the shed was locked. However, there was a window, and that window could be easily slid back. Ruth shrank from attempting to creep in by it.

"Just the same, I told him I'd get it—at least, I told myself I'd get it for him," thought the girl of the Red Mill. "And I will."

Of course, Mrs. Tingley would have allowed her to borrow the tool, but it would have aroused comment had it become known that Jerry wanted it.

Alice B. Emerson

"It must be that he really thinks now he knows where his uncle hid the treasure box. He wants to dig for it," was Ruth's thought.

Yet she remembered that Jerry had said all along the old man had seemingly gone mad because his treasure box was buried under a landslide. She asked Mr. Preston, the foreman of the camp, where the landslide had occurred.

"Why, right over yonder, little lady," explained the woods-man. "If the snow wasn't on the ground, you could easy see the scar of it down that hillside," and he pointed to a spot just beyond the secret opening of Jerry's cave.

"The dirt and rock was heaped up so at the foot of the slide that the course of the brook was changed. That slide covered a monster lot of little caves in the rock," pursued the man. "But I expect there's others of 'em left and that Jerry's hidin' out in one now," he added, looking at Ruth with shrewd gaze.

Ruth took him no further into her confidence. She felt that she must have somebody to help her, however, and naturally enough she chose Tom. Helen's twin thought a great deal of Ruth Fielding, and was never ashamed of showing this feeling before the other boys. On her side, Ruth felt that Tom Cameron was just about right.

Nor was she mistaken in him when she placed her difficulty before the lad. Help her? Of course he would! They agreed to make the raid upon the toolshed that evening when the others were busily filling stockings and trimming the huge Christmas tree set up in the main hall of the hunting lodge.

Ruth beckoned to her fellow-conspirator and Tom slipped out of the hall by one door while she made the outer air by another. The kitchen girls and the men hired about the camp were all in the big hall watching the fun, or aiding in decorating the lodge. Nobody saw Ruth and Tom.

It was a very cold evening. There was a hazy moon and brilliant stars, but they did not think anybody would see their efforts to aid Jerry Sheming.

Nevertheless, Ruth and Tom were very circumspect. They crept behind the toolshed and looked all about to make sure that nobody was watching. There was no light in the bunkhouse or in the cook's cabin.

Although the toolshed was so carefully locked, Ruth knew that the window could be opened. Tom quickly slipped back the sash, and then dived into the dark interior of the place, head first.

The moment he was on his feet, however, he drew from his pocket the electric spotlight he had supplied himself with, and flashed the ray about the shed.

"Good! here's either one you want—pickax or mattock," were the words he whispered to Ruth.

"Which do you suppose he would like best?"

"A mattock is more practical, I believe," said Tom. "'Maddox,' they call it. We had a fellow working for us once who called it a 'mad-ax.' It has a broad blade and can be used to chop as well as dig."

"Never mind giving a lecture on it," laughed Ruth, very softly, "hand it out."

Tom chuckled and did as he was bid. In a minute he was

Alice B. Emerson

with her and picked up the heavy implement.

"I hope they don't come hunting for us," said the girl of the Red Mill, breathlessly.

"We must take that risk. Come on, Ruth. Or do you want me to take it down to the brookside alone?"

"I want to go along, too. Oh, dear! I do hope he will find it."

"I have another cracker box full of food for him," said Tom. "I reckon he will be on the lookout for the pick, so he'll find the food, too."

After a good deal of climbing, they reached the flat rock by the brookside where Jerry Sheming had requested Ruth to leave the mattock. There was no sign of the fugitive about. Ruth did not tell Tom where the mouth of the secret tunnel lay—nor did Tom ask for information.

As they hurried back, mounting the ridge that separated the lodge and its outbuildings from the middle of the island, Ruth, looking back, suddenly grabbed Tom's hand.

"See! see there!" she cried.

Tom looked in the direction to which she pointed. The stars gave light enough for them to see miles across the ice. Several black figures were hurrying toward the western end of the island from the direction of the mainland—the southern shore of the lake.

"Who do you suppose those men are?" asked Ruth, faintly.

Tom shook his head slowly. "I expect it's Lem Daggett, the constable, and others to hunt for poor Jerry. I feel almost sure that the man in the lead is Daggett."

"Isn't that mean?" exclaimed Ruth, her voice shaking.

"It is. But I don't believe they will find Jerry very easily."

Just the same, Ruth was not to be comforted. She was very quiet all the rest of the evening. Her absence, and Tom's, had not been noticed. The crowd went to bed before eleven, having spent a most delightful Christmas Eve.

Ruth sat at a window that overlooked a part of the island. Once she saw the men who had crossed from the mainland climbing the hill toward the lone pine.

"I hope they won't find a trace of him!" she murmured as she popped into bed.

Ruth slept as soundly as any of her mates. A clanging bell at six o'clock aroused the whole household. The sun was not yet up, but there was a streak of gold across the eastern sky. It was Christmas morning.

Ruth ran again to the west window. A pillar of smoke rose straight from a hollow on the higher part of the island. The searching party was still there.

There was no time now to think of Jerry Sheming and his affairs. The girls raced to see who should dress first. Downstairs there were "loads" of presents waiting for them, so Belle declared.

"Come on!" cried Heavy, leading the way. "Ready all? March!"

The nine girls started through the hall and down the broad

stairway in single file. Heavy began to cheer and the others chimed in:

> "'S.B.—Ah-h-h!
> S.B.—Ah-h-h!
> Sound our battle-cry
> Near and far!
> S.B.—All!
> Briarwood Hall!
> Sweetbriars, do or die—
> This be our battle-cry—
> Briarwood Hall!
> *That's All*!'"

So sounding the Sweetbriars' challenge, they met the grinning boys at the foot of the flight, before the huge, sparkling tree.

"Gee!" exclaimed Tom. "I'm mighty glad I suggested that name for your secret society, Ruth. 'Sweetbriars'—it just fits you."

CHAPTER XVIII

FUN ON THE ICE

Of course, the girls had prepared one another's presents long before. Each had been tied in a queer bundle so, in trimming the tree, the nature of the contents could not be guessed.

The oddest shaped things hung from the branches of the Christmas tree, and the boys had excelled in making up these "surprise packages." Mrs. Tingley handed the presents out, while the boys lifted them down for her. A long, tightly rolled parcel, which looked as though it ought to contain an umbrella, and was marked "To Helen from Tom," finally proved to contain a jeweler's box, in which nestled a pretty ring, which delighted his twin.

A large, flat package, big enough to hold a large kite, was carefully opened by Belle, who finally found in it, among the many tissue wrappings, a pretty set of hair combs set with stones. In a roughly-done-up parcel was a most disreputable old shoe addressed to Lluella. She was going to throw it out, but the boys advised her so strongly not to that she finally burrowed to the toe and found, to her amazement, a gold bracelet.

There was a good-sized box for Ann Hicks—just as it had

Alice B. Emerson

come from the express office at Lumberton a week before. Having been addressed in Mrs. Tellingham's care, the western girl had known nothing about it.

Now it was opened last. It had come all the way from Silver Ranch, of course. Such a set of furs no girl at Briarwood possessed. There were a number of other presents from the cowboys, from Mrs. Sally, and from Bashful Ike himself. Ann was so pleased and touched that she ran away to hide her tears.

There were presents for each of the girls and boys who had been at Bullhide the previous summer. Bill Hicks had forgotten nobody, and, as Mrs. Tellingham had once said, the ranchman certainly was a generous man.

No member of the house party was overlooked on this bright Christmas morning. Mercy's presents were as costly and numerous as those of any other girl. Besides, the lame girl had been able to give her mates beautiful little keepsakes that expressed her love for them quite as much as would have articles that cost more money.

Her presents to the boys were funny, including a jumping jack on a stick to Isadore, the face of which Mercy had whittled out and painted to look a good deal like the features of that active youth.

For two hours the young folk reveled in their presents. Then suddenly Heavy smelled the breakfast coffee and she led the charge to the long dining room. They were in the midst of the meal when Mr. Tingley himself arrived, having reached Logwood on the early train and driven across the ice in a sleigh.

The Tingley young people met him hilariously. He was a

big, bewhiskered man, with a jolly laugh and amiable manner. His eye could flash, too, if need be, Ruth judged. And almost at once she had an opportunity of seeing him stern.

"What crowd is that over at the west end of the island?" he asked his wife. "I see they have a fire. There must be four or five men there. Is it some of Blent's doings?"

"Oh, Dad!" cried Ralph Tingley, eagerly. "You ought to stop that. Those fellows are hunting Jerry Sheming."

"Who is Jerry Sheming?" he asked, quickly.

Mrs. Tingley explained briefly.

"I remember now," said her husband. "And this is the young lady who spoke a good word for the boy in the first place?" and he beckoned the eager Ruth to them. "What have you to say for your protege now, Miss?"

"Everything that is good," declared the girl of the Red Mill, quickly. "I am sure he is not at all the sort of boy this man Blent would have you believe. And perhaps, Mr. Tingley, his old uncle *may* have had some title to a part of this island."

"That puts *me* in bad, then—eh?" chuckled Mr. Tingley.

"Unless Mr. Blent has cheated you, sir," suggested Ruth, hesitatingly.

"He's a foxy old fellow. But I believe I have safeguarded myself. This trouble about something being buried on the island—Well! I don't know about that."

"I believe Jerry really has some idea now where his uncle put

Alice B. Emerson

the box. Even if the old hunter *was* crazy, he might have had some valuables. And surely Jerry has a better right to the box than Blent," Ruth said, indignantly.

"I'll see about that. Just as soon as I have had breakfast, I'll take Preston and go over and interview this gang of Blent's henchmen. I am not at all sure that he has any right to hunt the boy down, warrant or no warrant!"

That was when he looked grim and his eyes flashed. Ruth felt that her friend's father was just the man to give Jerry Sheming a fair deal if he had the chance.

When the boys proposed getting out the two iceboats and giving the girls a sail (for the wind was fresh), Ruth was as eager as the others to join in the sport.

Not all the girls would trust themselves to the scooters, but there were enough who went down to the ice to make an exceedingly hilarious party.

Ralph Tingley and Tom Cameron were the best pilots. The small iceboats were built so that two passengers could ride beside the steersman and sheet tender. So the girls took turns in racing up and down the smooth ice on the south side of the island.

Ruth and Helen liked to go together with Tom, who had Busy Izzy to tend sheet. It was "no fair" if one party traveled farther than from the dock to the mouth of the creek and back again.

The four friends—Ruth and her chum, and Tom and Busy Izzy—were making their second trip over the smooth course. Bobbins, with his sister and The Fox, and Ralph Tingley, manned the other boat.

The two swift craft had a splendid race to the mouth of that brook which, because of its swiftness, still remained unshackled by the frost. The shallow stream of water poured down over the rocks into the lake, but there was only a small open place at the point where the brook emptied into its waters into the larger and more placid body.

When the two iceboats swung about, the one Bobbins manned got away at once and swiftly passed down the lake. The sheet fouled in Tom's boat. Busy Izzy had to drop the sail and the boat was brought to a halt.

"There are Mr. Tingley and Preston going over to talk to the constable and his crowd," remarked Isadore. "See yonder?"

"I hope he sends those men off the island. I don't see what right they have here, anyway," Helen exclaimed.

"If only Jerry knows enough to keep under cover while they are here," said Tom, looking meaningly at Ruth. They both wondered if the fugitive had ventured out of his cave to find the mattock and box of food they had left for him the evening before.

The craft was under way again in a minute or two, and they swept down the course in the wake of the other boat. Suddenly the sharp crack of a rifle echoed across the island. Helen screamed. Ruth risked the boom and sat up to look behind.

"There's a fight!" yelled Busy Izzy. "I believe they're after Jerry."

They saw Mr. Tingley and Preston hastening their steps toward the brook. As the iceboat swept out farther from the shore, the four friends aboard her could see several men running in the same direction. One bore a smoking gun in his hand.

"Right towards that rock, Ruthie!" gasped Tom, venturing a glance behind him.

"What rock do you mean?" demanded his sister.

"The rock where you folks found me the other day. It's near the opening to Jerry's cave. I see them!"

"'Ware boom!" yelled Tom, and shifted his helm.

The great sail went slowly over; the iceboat swooped around like a great bird skimming the ice. Then, in a minute, it was headed back up the lake toward the scene of the trouble.

Another rifle shot echoed across the ice.

CHAPTER XIX

BLENT IS MASTER

Ruth was truly frightened, and so was her chum. Could it be possible that those rough men dared fire their guns at Jerry Sheming? Or was the poor boy foolish enough to try to frighten his pursuers off with the weapons which Ruth very well knew he had in the cave with him?

"Oh, I'm glad Mr. Tingley's here to-day," cried Busy Izzy. "He'll give that Lem Daggett what's coming to him—that's what *he'll* do!"

"Hope so," agreed Tom, grimly.

The latter brought the iceboat into the wind near the shore, and Isadore dropped the sail again. They all tumbled out and ran up the bank. A little climb brought them to the plateau where they could see all that was going on near the rock on which Ruth and Tom had left the mattock the evening before.

Lem Daggett had four men with him—all rough-looking fellows, and armed with rifles. Jerry Sheming was standing half-leg deep in the running stream, his hands over his head, and the men were holding him under the muzzles of their guns.

"Why! it beats the 'wild and woolly'!" gasped Tom Cameron. "Silver Ranch and Bullhide weren't as bad as this. The scoundrels!"

"Come out o' that brook, Jerry, or it'll be the wuss for ye." Lem Daggett drawled, standing on the flat rock and grinning at his captive.

"What do you want of me?" demanded the fugitive, sullenly.

"You know well enough. Oh, I got a warrant for ye, all right. Ev'rything's all right an' proper. Ye know Rufe Blent don't make no mistakes. He's got ye."

"An' here he comes now!" ejaculated another of the rough men, looking toward the east end of the island.

The four hurrying young folk looked back. Driving hastily from the lodge, and behind Mr. Tingley and Preston, came a heavy sleigh drawn by a pair of horses. Rufus Blent and a driver were in it.

But Mr. Tingley approached first, and it was plain by a single glance at his face that he was angry.

"What's all this shooting about?" he demanded. "Don't you men know that Cliff Island is private property? You are trespassing upon it."

"Oh, I guess we're within our rights, boss," said Lem Daggett, laughing. "I'm the constable. And these here are helpers o' mine. We was arter a bird, and we got him."

"A warrant from a justice of the peace does not allow you to go out with guns and rifles and shoot over private property," declared Mr. Tingley, angrily. "Be off with you—and don't you dare come to this island again without permission."

"Hold on, thar!" yelled Rufus Blent, leaping from the sleigh with more agility than one would have given him credit for. "You air oversteppin' the line, Mr. Tingley. That officer's in the right."

"No, he's not in the right. He'd never be in the right—hunting a boy with an armed posse. I should think you and these other men would be ashamed of yourselves."

"You look out, Mr. Tingley," warned Blent, hotly. "You're a stranger in these parts. You try to balk me and you'll be sorry."

"Why?" demanded the city man, quite as angrily. "Are you the law and the prophets here, Mr. Blent?"

"I know my rights. And if you want to live in peace here, keep out o' my way!" snarled the real estate man.

"You old scoundrel!" exclaimed Mr. Tingley, stepping swiftly toward him. "Get off Cliff Island—and get off quick. I'd spend a thousand dollars to get a penny's worth of damages from you. I'll sue you in the civil courts for trespass if you don't go—and go quick!

"Don't think I went blindly into the transaction that gave me title to this island. I know all about your withholding the right to 'treasure trove,' and all that. But it doesn't give you the right to trespass here. Get out—and take your gang with you—or I'll have suit begun against you at once."

Old Blent was troubled, but he had one good hold and he

Alice B. Emerson

knew it. He shouted to Lem Daggett:

"Serve that warrant, Lem, and come along. Bring that young rascal. I'll fix him."

"Let me read that warrant!" exclaimed Mr. Tingley, suddenly.

"No, ye don't!" yelled Blent. "Don't let him take it into his hand. Read it aloud to him. But make that pesky young Sheming come ashore first. Before ye know it, he'll be runnin' away ag'in."

The men who "covered" Jerry motioned him to step up to the bank. They looked so threatening that he obeyed. Daggett produced a legal looking paper. He read this aloud, blunderingly, for he was an illiterate man.

Its contents were easily gathered, however. Squire Keller had signed the warrant on complaint of Rufus Blent. Jerry was accused of having stolen several boxes of ammunition and a revolver. The property had been found in an old shed at Logwood where the boy had slept for a few nights after he had first been driven from Cliff Island.

"Why, this is an old story, Blent," ejaculated Mr. Tingley, angrily. "The boy left that shed months ago. He came directly to the island, when I hired him, from the neighborhood of Lumberton, and Preston assures me he hasn't been to Logwood since arriving."

"You can tell all that in court," snarled Blent, waving his hand. "If he's got witnesses to clear him, I guess they'll be given a chance to testify."

"You're a villain!" declared the city man.

"Lemme tell you something, Mr. Tingley. There's a law to punish callin' folks out o' their names! I know the law, an' don't you forget it. Come here, you, Jerry Sheming! Git in this sleigh. And you, too, Lem. You other fellers can come back to Logwood and I'll pay ye as I agreed."

Ruth had, meanwhile, met Jerry when he came ashore. She seized his hand and, almost in tears, told him how sorry she was he was captured.

"Don't you mind, Miss Ruth. He's bound to git me out of the way if he can," whispered Jerry. "Rufe Blent is *all* the law there is in Logwood, I guess."

"But Mr. Tingley will help you."

"Maybe. But if Blent can't prove this hatched up business against me, he'll keep right on persecuting me, if I don't light out. An' I believe I found something, Miss Ruth."

"Your uncle's money?"

"I wouldn't say that. But I was goin' to break into another little cave if I'd got hold of that mattock. The mouth is under the debris that fell with the landslide. It was about where Uncle Pete said he hid his treasure box. Poor Uncle Pete! Losin' that box was what sent him off his head complete, like."

This had been said too low for the others to hear. But now Daggett came forward and clamped his big paw on Jerry's shoulder.

"Come along, you!" commanded the constable, jerking his prisoner toward the sledge.

"Oh, isn't it a mean, mean shame?" cried Helen Cameron.

"Wish that old Blent was my size," grumbled Busy Izzy, clenching his fists and glaring at the real estate man.

"I wish I could do something at the present moment to help you, Sheming," said Mr. Tingley, his expression very angry. "But don't be afraid. You have friends. I shall come right over to Keller's court, and I shall hire a lawyer to defend you."

"You kin do all ye like," sneered Blent, as the sledge started with the prisoner. "But I'll beat ye. And ye'll pay for tryin' to balk me, too."

"Don't you be too loose with your threats, Rufe," sang out Preston, the foreman. "If anything happens over here on the island—any of Mr. Tingley's property is destroyed—we'll know who to look to for damages."

"Yah!" snarled Blent, and drove away.

The fact remained, however, that, for the time being at least, Rufus Blent was master of the situation.

CHAPTER XX

THE FISHING PARTY

Ruth felt so unhappy she wept openly. It seemed too bad that Jerry Sheming should be taken away to the mainland a prisoner.

"They'll find some way of driving him out of this country again," remarked Preston, the foreman. "You don't know Blent, Mr. Tingley, as well as the rest of us do. Other city men have come up here and bucked against him in times past—and they were sorry before they got through."

"What do you mean?" demanded the angry owner of Cliff Island.

"Blent can hire those fellows from the lumber camps, and some of the guides, to do his dirty work. That's all I've got to say. Hunting camps have burned down in these woods before now," observed the foreman, significantly.

"Why! the scoundrel sold me this island himself!"

"And he's sold other outsiders camp sites. But they have had to leave if they angered Blent."

"He is a dangerous man, then?"

"Well—things just happen," returned Preston, shaking his head. "I'd keep watch if I were you."

"I will. I'll hire guards—and arm 'em, if need be," declared Mr. Tingley, emphatically. "But take it from me—I am going to see that that boy Jerry is treated right in these backwoods courts. That's the way I feel about it."

Ruth was glad to hear him say this. As she had decided when she first saw him, Mr. Tingley could be very firm if he wished to be. At once he went back to the house, had a team hitched to a sleigh, and drove over to the mainland so as to be sure that Blent did not get ahead of him and have court convened before the proper hour.

The day was spoiled for Ruth and for some of the other young folk who had taken such a deep interest in Jerry. The boy had been caught because he tried to get the mattock Ruth and Tom had put out for him. Ruth wished now that she and Tom had not gone down to the brook.

There was too much going on at Cliff Island for even Ruth to mope long. Mr. Tingley came back at dark and said he had succeeded in getting Jerry's case put over until a lawyer could familiarize himself with the details. Meanwhile Keller, Blent's man, had refused to accept bail. Jerry would have to remain in jail for a time.

A man came across from the town that evening and brought a telegram for Mr. Tingley. That gentleman had without doubt shown his interest in Jerry Sheming. Fearing that the local legal lights might be somewhat backward about opposing Rufus Blent, he had telegraphed to his own firm of lawyers in New York and they were sending him a reputable attorney from an up-State city who would be at Logwood the next day.

"Let's all go over to court to-morrow and see that lawyer get Jerry free," suggested Belle Tingley, and the others agreed with enthusiasm. It would be as much fun as snow-shoeing; more fun for those who had not already learned that art.

The day after Christmas, in the morning, the boys insisted that everybody but Mercy Curtis should get out and try the shoes. Those who had been at Snow Camp the year before were able to set out quite briskly—for it is an art that, like swimming and skating, is not easily forgotten.

There were some very funny spills and by luncheon they were all in a glow. Later the big sledge was brought around and behind that the boys strung a couple of bobs. The horses drew them down to the ice and there it was easy for the team to pull the whole crowd across to Logwood.

The town seemed to have turned out to meet the party from Cliff Island.

Ruth and her friends noted the fact that many of the half-grown boys and young men—those of the rougher class—seemed greatly amused by the appearance of the city folk.

"But what can you expect from a lot of rubes?" demanded Tom, rather angrily. "See 'em snickering and grinning? What d'ye s'pose is the matter with them?"

"Whatever the joke is, it's on us and we don't know it," remarked Heavy, who was easily angered by ridicule, too. "There! Mr. Tingley has gone off with the lawyer. I guess we'll know what it's all about pretty soon."

Alice B. Emerson

And *that* was true, sure enough. It came out that there would be no case to try. Justice Keller announced that the accusation against Jerry Sheming had been withdrawn. Mr. Blent had "considered Mr. Tingley's plea for mercy," the old fox said, and there was nothing the justice could do but to turn the prisoner loose.

"But what's become of him?" Mr. Tingley wanted to know.

"Oh, that does not enter into my jurisdiction," replied Keller, blandly. "I am not his keeper. He was let out of jail early this morning. After that I cannot say what became of him."

Blent was not even at the court. It was learned that he had gone out of town. Blent could always find somebody to handle pitch for him.

It was later discovered that when Lem Daggett had opened the jail to Jerry, several of Blent's ruffians had rushed the boy to the railroad yard, put him aboard a moving freight, given a brakeman a two-dollar bill as per instructions from the real estate man, and Jerry wasn't likely to get off the train, unless he jumped while it was moving, until it was fifty miles farther west.

But, of course, this story did not come out right away. The whole town was laughing at Mr. Tingley. Nobody cared enough about the city man, or knew him well enough, to explain the details of Jerry's disappearance at that time.

Mr. Tingley looked very serious when he rejoined the young folk and he had little to say on the way home, save to Ruth, whom he beckoned to the seat beside him.

"I am very sorry that the old fox got the best of us, Miss Fielding. As Preston says, I must look out for him. He is sly, wicked, and powerful. My Albany lawyer tells me that Blent is notorious in this part of the State, and that he has great political influence, illiterate as he is.

"But I am going to fight. I have bought Cliff Island, and paid a good price for it. I have spent a good many thousand dollars in improvements already. I'll protect myself and my investment if I can—and meanwhile I'll do what I can for your friend, Jerry Sheming, too.

"They've got the boy away from the vicinity for the time being, but I reckon he'll find his way back. You think so, too, Miss Fielding?"

"If he understands that we are trying to help him. And— yes!—I believe he will come back anyway, for he is very anxious to find that treasure box his Uncle Peter lost."

"Oh—as to that—Well, there may be something in it. But Pete Tilton was really insane. I saw him myself. The asylum is the place for him, poor man," concluded Mr. Tingley.

Ruth felt in secret very much worried over Jerry's disappearance. When she once became interested in anybody, as Helen said, "she was interested all the way through."

The others could laugh a little about how the crafty real estate agent had fooled Mr. Tingley and gotten Jerry out of the way, but not Ruth. She could scarcely sleep that night for thinking of what might have happened to the ill-used youth.

But she tried to hide her anxiety from her companions the next morning when plans were made for a fishing trip. All but Mercy joined in this outing. They went on snowshoes to the far end of the island, keeping on the beach under the huge cliffs, to a little cove where they would be sheltered

Alice B. Emerson

and where the fishing was supposed to be good.

Preston, the foreman, went with them. He and the boys dragged a bobsled well laden with the paraphernalia considered necessary for fishing through the ice.

First the holes were cut—thirteen of them. Then, near each hole, and on the windward side, two stakes were set about four feet apart and a square of canvas lashed between them for a wind-break. A folding campstool had been brought for each fisherman and "fishergirl," and there were a lot of old sacks for the latter, especially, to put under their feet as they watched the "bobbers" in the little pool of water before which they sat.

After Preston saw them well started, he went back to the house. The crowd intended to remain until evening, and planned to make their dinner on the shore of the cove, frying some of the fish they expected to catch, and making coffee in a battered camp pot that had been brought along.

The fish were there, as the foreman had assured them. Each member of the party watched and baited two lines. At first some of the girls had considerable trouble with the bait, and the boys had to show them how to put it on the hook; but it was fun, and soon all were interested in pulling out the flopping fish, vying with each other in the catch, calling back and forth about their luck, and having a splendid time.

It was so cold that the fish froze almost as soon as they were thrown upon the ice. Had they been catching for shipment, the fish could have been boxed and sent some distance by express without being iced.

But the young folk did not mind the cold much, nor the fact that the sun did not shine and the clouds grew thicker as the day advanced.

"I'm going to beat you all!" declared The Fox, after a great run of luck, in which she could scarcely bait rapidly enough to satisfy the ravenous fish. "Might as well award me the laurel wreath right now."

"Don't you be too sure," drawled Heavy. "You know, 'He laughs best who laughs last.'"

"Wrong!" returned Mary Cox. "The true quotation should be, 'He laughs best whose laugh lasts.' And mine is going to last—oh-he! here comes another!"

Tom and Ruth got the dinner. There was plenty of dry wood under the fir trees. Tom cleaned the fish and Ruth fried them to a delicious brownness and crispness. With the other viands brought from home and cups of good, hot coffee, the thirteen friends made a hearty and hilarious meal.

They were sheltered by the high cliff at their backs and did not notice when the snow began to fall. But, after a time, they suddenly discovered that the flakes were coming so thick and fast that it was all but impossible to see the farthest fishing shelters.

"Oh, dear me! we don't want to go back yet," wailed The Fox. "And we were catching them so fast. Do, do let's wait a while longer."

"Not much fun if it keeps on snowing this way," objected Bobbins.

"Don't begin croaking, little boy," advised his sister. "A few flakes of snow won't hurt us."

Alice B. Emerson

Nevertheless, the storm did not hold up. It was more than a "flurry" and some of the others, as well as Bob Steele, began to feel anxious.

CHAPTER XXI

JERRY'S CAVE

For a while they tried to shelter themselves with the canvas, and shouted back and forth through the falling snow that they were having a "scrumptious" time. But some of the girls, as Isadore said, "began to weaken."

"We don't want to be lost in the snow as we were the time we went for balsam at Snow Camp," said Helen.

"How can you get lost—with us fellows along?" demanded Busy Izzy, in vast disgust.

"Can't a boy be lost?" demanded Ann Hicks, laughing.

"Not on your life!" declared the irrepressible Isadore.

But just then Madge Steele got up and declared she had had enough. "This hole in the ice is filling up with snow. We'll lose the fish we've already caught if we don't look out. Come on, Bobby, and get mine."

So it was agreed to cut the fishing short for that day, although The Fox declared she could have beaten them all in another hour.

Alice B. Emerson

However, they had a great load of the frozen fish. Besides what they had eaten for dinner, there were at least a hundred handsome fellows, and the boys had strung each fisher's catch on a birch twig which they had cut and trimmed while coming down to the lake that morning.

Tom and Ruth, left at the campfire to clean up after the midday meal, were shouting for them to come in. The girls left the boys to wind up the fishlines and "strike camp," as Ralph called taking down the pieces of canvas, and all hustled for the shore. They crowded around the fire, threw on more fuel, danced to get their feet warm, and called to the boys to hurry.

The five boys had their hands full in retrieving all the chairs, and canvas sheets, and fish lines, and sacks. When they got them all in and packed upon the bobsled for transportation, the snow was a foot deep on the ice and it was snowing so fast that one could not see ten feet into the swirling heart of the storm.

"I declare! it looks as though we were in a mess, with all this snow," complained Tom Cameron.

"And with all these girls," growled Ralph Tingley. "Wish we'd started an hour ago."

"I don't know about starting *at all*," observed Bobbins. "Don't you see that the girls will give out before we're half-way there? We can't use snowshoes with the snow coming down like this. They clog too fast."

"Oh, they'll have to wade the same as we do," said Isadore.

"Yah! Wade! And us pulling this sled, too? I wish Preston had stayed with us. Don't you, Ralph?" asked his brother.

"Hush! don't let the girls hear you," was the whispered reply.

Already the girls were comparing notes in a group around the fire. Now Madge turned and shouted for them:

"Come here, boys! Don't be mumbling together there. We have an idea."

"If it's any good, let's have it," answered Tom, cheerfully.

"It is good. It was born of experience. Some of us got all the tramping in a blinding snowstorm that we wanted a year ago. Never again! Eh, girls?"

"Quite right, Madge," said Ralph. "It is foolish to run into danger. We are all right here—"

"Why, the snow will drown out your fire in half an hour," scoffed Isadore. "And there isn't so much dry fuel."

"I know where there is plenty of wood—and shelter, too!" cried Ruth, suddenly.

"So do I. At the lodge," scoffed Belle.

"No. Nearby. Tom and I were just talking about it. Up that ravine yonder is the place where I fell over the cliff. And Jerry's cave is right there—one end of it."

"A cave!" ejaculated Helen. "That would be bully."

"If only we could have a good fire and get dry and warm again," quoth Lluella, her teeth already chattering.

"I believe that would be best," admitted Madge Steele. "We never could get back to the lodge through this snow. The shore is so rough."

"We can travel on the ice," ventured Ann Hicks, doubtfully.

"And get turned around," put in Tom. "Easiest thing in the world to get lost out there on that ice without a compass and in such a whirlwind of snow. Ruth's right. Let's try to find the cave."

"I'm game!" exclaimed Heavy. "Why, with all this fish we could live a week in a cave. It would be bully."

"'Charming' is the better word, Miss Stone," suggested The Fox.

"Don't correct me when I'm on a vacation," exclaimed the plump girl. "I won't stand for it—"

Just then she slipped and sat down hard and they all laughed.

"Lucky you weren't on the ice. You'd gone right through that time, Jennie," declared The Fox. "Now, let's come on to the cave if we're all agreed. I guess Ruth has the right idea."

"We'll drag the sled and break a path for you girls," announced Tom. "All ready, now! Bring your snowshoes. If it stops snowing, we can get home on them to-night."

"Oh, dear, me! I hope so," cried Belle Tingley. "What will mother and father say if we're not home by dark?"

"They'll be pretty sure we wouldn't travel far in this storm. Preston and the other men will find us, anyway."

"I expect that is so," admitted Ruth, thoughtfully, "And they'll find Jerry's cave. I hope he won't be mad at me for taking you all there."

However that might be, it seemed to the girl of the Red Mill, as well as to Tom Cameron, that it was wisdom to seek the nearest shelter. The ravine was steep, but it was sheltered. There were not many big drifts until they reached that great one at the head of it, into which Ruth had fallen when she slipped over the brink of the precipice.

Nevertheless, they were half an hour beating their way up the gully and out upon that ledge which led to the mouth of Jerry's cave. The boys found the laden sled a good deal of a load and the girls had all they could do to follow in the track the sled made.

"We never *could* have reached home safely through this storm," declared Madge. "How clever of you to remember the cave, Ruthie."

"Ruth is always doing something clever," said Helen, loyally. "Why, she even falls over a cliff, so as to find a cave that, later, shelters us all from the inclement elements."

"Wow, wow, wow!" jeered Isadore. "You girls think a lot of each other; don't you? Better thank that Jerry boy for finding the cave in the first place."

They were all crowding into the place by this time. It was not very light in the cave, for the snow had already veiled the entrance. But there was a great store of wood piled up along one side, and the boys soon had a fresh fire built.

The girls and boys stamped off the clinging snow and began to feel more comfortable. The flames danced among the sticks, and soon an appreciable sense of warmth stole through the cave. The crowd began to laugh and chatter. The

Alice B. Emerson

girls brushed out the cave and the boys rolled forward loose stones for seats.

Isadore found Jerry's shotgun, ammunition, bow and arrow, and other possessions.

"He must have taken the rifle with him when he went to the other end of the tunnel," Ruth said.

"Say!" exclaimed Ralph Tingley. "You could find the way through the hill to where you came out of the cave with Jerry; couldn't you, Ruth?"

"Oh! I believe so," cried Ruth.

"Then we needn't worry," said the boy. "We can go home that way. Even if the storm doesn't stop to-night, we ought to be able to find the lodge from *that* end of the cave."

"We've nothing to worry about, then," said Madge, cheerfully. "We're supplied with all the comforts of home—"

"And plenty to eat," sighed Heavy, with satisfaction.

CHAPTER XXII

SNOWED IN

Naturally, thirteen young folk in a cave could not be content to sit before the fire inactive. They played games, they sang songs, they made up verses, and finally Madge produced a pencil and a notebook and they wrote a burlesque history of "George Washington and the Cherry Tree."

The first author wrote a page of the history and two lines on the second page. Then the second read those last two lines and went on with the story, leaving another two lines at the top of the next page, and so on. It was a wonderful piece of literary work when it was finished, and Madge kept it to read to the S.B.'s when they got back to Briarwood Hall.

"For, of course," she said, "we're not going to be forever shut up in this cave. I don't want to turn into a 'cave man'—nor yet a 'cave woman'!"

"See if the snow has stopped—that's a good boy, Tommy," urged Helen.

"Of course it hasn't. Don't you see how dark it is, sis?" returned her twin.

Alice B. Emerson

But he started toward the mouth of the cavern. Just then Bob looked at his watch in the firelight, and exclaimed:

"No wonder it seems dark—do you know it's half after four right now?"

"Wow! mother will be scared," said Ralph Tingley.

Just then there came a cry from Tom. Then followed a heavy, smothered thud. The boys dashed to the entrance. It was pitch dark. A great mass of hard packed snow filled the opening, and was being forced into the cave itself. In this heap of snow struggled Tom, fairly smothered.

They laid hold upon him—by a leg and an arm—and dragged him out. He could not speak for a moment and he had lost his cap.

"How did you do that?" demanded Bob. "What does it mean?"

"Think—think I did it on purpose?" demanded the overwhelmed youth. "I'm no Samson to pull down the pillars on top of me. Gee! that snow came sudden."

"Where—where did it all come from?" demanded his sister.

"From the top of the cliff, of course. It must have made a big drift there and tumbled down—regular avalanche, you know —just as I tried to look out. Why! the place out there is filled up yards deep! We'd never be able to dig out in a week."

"Oh, dear me! what shall we do?" groaned Belle, who was beginning to get nervous.

"Have supper," suggested Heavy, calmly. "No matter what

we have to face, we can do it better after eating."

They laughed, but took her advice. Nobody failed to produce an appetite at the proper time.

"Dear me!" exclaimed Belle, "if only mother knew we were safe I'd be content to stay all night. It's fun."

"And if we had some salt," complained Lluella. "I don't like fish without salt—not much."

"You're a fine female Robinson Crusoe," laughed Tom. "This is real 'roughing it.' I expect all you girls will weaken by morning."

"Oh, oh!" cried his sister, "you talk as though you thought we would be obliged to stay here, Tom."

"I don't just see how we're to get out to-night," Tom returned, grimly. "Not from this end of the cave, at any rate. I tell you, tons and *tons* of snow fell into its mouth."

"But you know the other way out, Ruthie?" urged Lluella, half inclined to cry.

"I think so," returned the girl of the Red Mill.

"Then just hunt for the way," said Belle, firmly. "If it has stopped snowing I want to go home."

"Don't be a baby, Belle," advised her brother Ralph. "Nothing is going to hurt us here."

"Especially as we have plenty of fuel and grub," added Bobbins, thoughtfully.

　　　　　Alice B. Emerson

But Ruth saw that it would be wiser to try to get through the tunnel to the brookside. Nobody could dig them out at this end, that was sure. So she agreed with Tom and Ralph Tingley to try to follow the same passages that Jerry Sheming had taken her through upon the occasion of her first visit.

"How shall we find our way, though, if it's dark?" questioned Ralph, suddenly. "*I* can't see in the dark."

"Neither can the rest of us, I guess," said Tom. "Do you suppose we could find torchwood in that pile yonder?"

"Not much," Bobbins told them. "And a torch is a smoky thing, anyway."

Ruth was hunting the dark corners of the big cavern in which they had camped. Although Jerry had been at the far end of the tunnel when he was captured by the constable and his helpers—outside that end of the tunnel, in fact—she hoped that he had left his lantern at this end.

As it proved, she was not mistaken. Here it was, all filled and cleaned, hidden on a shelf with a half-gallon can of kerosene. Jerry had been in the habit of coming to the cave frequently in the old days when his uncle and he lived alone on the island.

So Tom lit the lantern and the trio started. The opening of the tunnel through the hill could not be missed; but farther along Ruth had a dim recollection of passing cross galleries and passages. Should she know the direct tunnel then?

She put that anxiety aside for the present. At first it was all plain traveling, and Tom with the lantern went ahead to illuminate the path.

They came out into one of the narrow open cuts, but there was little snow in it. However, a flake or two floated down to them, and they knew that the storm still continued to rage. The moaning of the wind in the tree tops far up on the hill reached their ears.

"Some storm, this," observed Tom.

"I should say it was! You don't suppose the folks will be foolish enough to start out hunting for us till it's over; do you?" Ralph asked, anxiously.

"They would better not. We're safe. They ought to know that. Preston will tell them about the caves in this end of the island and they ought to know we'd find one of 'em."

"It's a wild spot, just the same," remarked Ralph. "And I suppose mother will be worried."

"Ruth isn't afraid—nor Helen—nor the other girls," said Tom. "I think these Briarwood girls are pretty plucky, any-way. Don't *you* get to grouching, Rafe."

They pursued their way, Tom ahead with the lantern, for some rods further. Suddenly the leader stopped.

"Now what, Ruthie?" he demanded. "Which way do we go?"

The passage forked. Ruth was uncertain. She could not for the life of her remember having seen this spot before.

But, then, she and Jerry must have passed it. She had not given her attention to the direction at that time, for she had been talking with the backwoods boy.

She took the lantern from Tom now, and walked a little way

Alice B. Emerson

into first the left-hand passage and then the right-hand one. It seemed to her as though there were places in the sand on the floor of this latter tunnel which had been disturbed by human feet.

"*This* is the path, I guess," she said, laughing and so hiding her own anxiety. "But let's take a good look at the place so we can find our way back to it if we have to return."

"Huh!" grumbled Ralph Tingley. "You're not so awfully sure; are you?"

"That's all right. Ruth was only through here once," Tom spoke up, loyally. "And we can't get really lost."

In five minutes they came into a little circular room out of which no less than four passages opened. Ruth was confident now that she was "turned around." She had to admit it to her companions.

"Well! what do you know about that?" cried Ralph. "I thought you said you could find the way?"

"I guess I can," said Ruth, cheerfully. "But we'll have to try each one of these openings. I can't be sure which is the right one."

Ralph sniffed, but Tom was unshaken in his confidence in his girl friend.

"Let me have the lantern, Tom, and you boys stay here," Ruth said, quickly. "I'll try them myself."

"Say! don't you get lost," cried Tom.

"And don't you leave us long in the dark," complained

Ralph. "I don't believe we ought to let her take that lantern, Tom—"

"Aw, stop croaking!" commanded young Cameron. "You're worse than any girl yourself, Tingley."

Ruth hated to hear them quarrel, but she would not give up and admit that she was beaten. She took the lantern and ventured into the first tunnel. Her carriage was firmer than her mind, and before she had gone a dozen steps she was nervously sobbing, but smothered the sounds with her handkerchief.

Alice B. Emerson

CHAPTER XXIII

"A BLOW FOR LIBERTY"

Ruth was a healthy girl and particularly free from "nerves"; but she *was* frightened. She was so proud that she determined not to admit to her companions that she was lost In the caves.

Indeed, she was not entirely sure that she *was* lost. Perhaps this was the way she had come with Jerry. Only, she did not remember passing the little room with the four tunnels opening out of it.

This first passage into which she had ventured with so much apparent boldness proved to be the wrong one within a very few moments. She came to the end of it—against an unbroken wall.

There she remained until she had conquered her nervous sobbing and removed as well as she could the traces of tears from her face. When she returned to Tom and Ralph she held the lantern well down, so that the shadow was cast upon her face.

"How about it, Ruth?" demanded Tom, cheerfully, when she reappeared.

"That's not the one. It is just a pocket," declared Ruth. "Wait till I try another."

"Well, don't be all night about it," growled Tingley, ungraciously. "We're wasting a lot of time here."

Ruth did not reply, but took the next tunnel. She followed this for even a shorter distance before finding it closed.

"Only two more. That's all right!" exclaimed Tom. "Narrows the choice down, and we'll be surer of hitting the right one— eh, Ruthie?"

She knew that he was talking thus to keep her courage up. Dear old Tom! he was always to be depended upon.

She gathered confidence herself, however, when she had gone some distance into the third passage. There was a place where she had to climb upon a shelf to get along, because the floor was covered with big stones, and she remembered this place clearly.

So she turned and swung her Tight, calling to the boys. Her voice went echoing through the tunnel and soon brought a reply and the sound of scrambling feet.

"Hold up that lantern!" yelled Ralph, rather crossly. "How do you expect us to see?"

Young Tingley's nerves were "on edge," and like a good many other people when they get that way, he was short-tempered.

"Now we're all right, are we, Ruth?" cried Tom.

"I remember this place," the girl of the Red Mill replied. "I couldn't be mistaken. Now you take the lantern, Tom, and lead on."

They pursued the tunnel to its very end. There it branched again and Ruth boldly took the right hand passage. Whether it was right, or no, she proposed to attack it firmly.

After a time Tom exclaimed: "Hullo, Ruthie! do you really think this is right?"

"What do you mean?"

He held up the lantern in silence. Ruth and Ralph crowded forward to look over his shoulders.

There was a heap of rubbish and earth half-filling the tunnel. It had not fallen from the roof, although neither that nor the sides of the tunnel were of solid rock.

"You never came through this place, Ruth!" exclaimed Ralph, in that "I-told-you-so" tone that is so hard to bear.

"I—I didn't see this place—no," admitted Ruth.

"Of course you didn't!" declared Ralph, crossly. "Why! it's right up against the end of the tunnel."

"It *does* look as though we were blocked, Ruthie," said Tom, with less confidence.

"Then we'll have to go back and try the other passage," returned the girl, choking a little.

"See here!" cried Tom, suddenly. "Somebody's been digging here. That's where all this stuff comes from, underfoot."

"Where?" asked the others, crowding forward to look closer. Tom set down the lantern and picked up a broken spade. There was a cavity in the wall of this pocket-like passage. With a flourish Tom dug the broken blade of the spade into the gritty earth.

"This is what Jerry wanted that mattock for, I bet!" he exclaimed.

"Oh, dear, me! do you believe so?" cried Ruth. "Then, right here, is where he thought he might find his uncle's treasure box."

"Ho, ho!" ejaculated Ralph. "That old hunter was just as crazy as he could be—father says so."

"Well, that wouldn't keep him from having money; would it?—and might be a very good reason for his burying it."

"And the papers he declared would prove his title to a part of this island," Ruth hastened to add.

That didn't please Ralph any too well. "My father owns the island, and don't you forget it!" he declared.

"Well, we don't have to quarrel about it," snapped Tom, rather disgusted with the way Ralph was behaving. "Come on! we might as well go back. But here's one blow for liberty!" and he laughed and flung the spade forward with all his strength.

Jerry Sheming had never suspected it, or he would not have left the excavation just as he had. There was but a thin shell beyond where he had been digging, and the spade in Tom's hand went clear through.

Alice B. Emerson

"For the goodness gracious grannies!" gasped Tom, scrambling off his knees. "I—I came near losing that spade altogether."

There was a fall of earth beyond the hole. They heard it rolling and tumbling down a sharp descent.

"Hold the lantern here, Ruth!" cried Tom, trying to peer into the opening.

Ruth did so. The rays revealed a hole, big enough for a man to creep through. It gave entrance, it seemed, to another cavern—and one of good size.

"Oh, my dear!" exclaimed Ruth, seizing Tom's arm. "I just know what this means."

"You may. *I* don't," laughed Tom Cameron.

"Why, this other cavern is the one that was buried under the landslide. Jerry said he knew about where it was, and he's been trying to dig into it."

"Oh, yes; there was a landslide on this side of the cliff just about the time father was negotiating for the purchase of the island last summer," said Ralph. "We all came up here to look at the place a while afterward. We camped in a tent about where the lodge now stands. That old crazy hunter had just been taken away from here. They say he tried to kill Blent."

"And maybe he had good reason," said Tom. "Blent is without a doubt a pretty mean proposition."

"Just the same, the island is my father's," declared Ralph, with confidence. "He bought it, right enough."

"All right. But you think, Ruth, that perhaps it was in this buried cave that old Mr. Tilton hid his money box?"

"So Jerry said. It looks as though Jerry had been digging here—"

"Let's have another crack at it!" cried Tom, and went to work with the spade again.

In ten minutes he had scattered considerable earth and made the hole much larger. They held the lantern inside and saw that the floor of the other cavity was about on a level with the one in which they stood. Tom slid the old spade through the hole, and then went through himself.

"Come on! let's take a look," he said, reaching up for Ruth and the lantern.

"But this isn't finding a way out," complained Ralph. "What will the other folks say?"

"We'll find the opening later. We couldn't venture outside now, anyway. It is still storming, you can bet," declared the eager Tom.

Ruth's sharp eyes were peering here and there. The cavern they had entered was almost circular and had a dome-shaped roof. There were shelves all around several feet above the floor. Some of these ledges slanted inward toward the rock, and one could not see much of them.

"Lift me up here, Tom!" commanded the girl. "I want to scramble up on the ledge."

"You'll hurt yourself."

Alice B. Emerson

"Nonsense! Can't I climb a tree almost as well as Ann Hicks?"

He gave her a lift and Ruth scrambled over the edge with a little squeal.

"Oh, oh, oh!" she cried. "Here's something."

"Must be," grunted Tom, trying to climb up himself. "Why, I declare, Ruthie! that's a box."

"It's a little chest. It's ironbound, too. My! how heavy. I can't lift it."

"Tumble it down and let's see," commanded Ralph, holding the lantern.

Ruth sat down suddenly and looked at the boys.

"I don't know," she said. "I don't know that we've got any right to touch it. It's padlocked. Maybe it is old Mr. Tilton's treasure-box."

"That would be great!" cried Tom.

"But I don't know," continued Ruth, reflectively. "We would better not touch it. I wouldn't undertake to advise Jerry what to do if *he* found it. But this is what they call 'treasure trove,' I guess. At least, it was what that Rufus Blent had in mind, all right, when he sold Mr. Tingley the island with the peculiar reservation clause in the deed."

CHAPTER XXIV

A MIDNIGHT MARAUDER

Meanwhile the boys and girls left behind in Jerry Sheming's old camp began to find the absence of Ruth and her two companions rather trying. The time which had elapsed since the three explorers started to find the eastern outlet of the cave seemed much longer to those around the campfire than to the trio themselves.

Before the searching party could have reached the brookside, had the tunnel been perfectly straight, the nervous Belle Tingley wanted to send out a relief expedition.

"We never should have allowed Ruthie to go," she wailed. "We all should have kept together. How do we know but they'll find the cave a regular labyrinth, and get lost in it, and wander around and around, and never find their way out, or back, and—"

"Oh, for the goodness sake!" ejaculated Mary Cox, "don't be such a weeping, wailing Sister of Misery, Belle! You not only cross bridges before you come to them, but, I declare, you build new ones!"

"She's Old Man Trouble's favorite daughter," said Heavy.

Alice B. Emerson

"Didn't you know *that*? Now, Miss Fuss-Budget, stop croaking. Nothing's going to happen to Ruthie."

"Not with Tom on hand, you can wager," added Helen, with every confidence in her twin brother.

But at last the watches of the party could not be doubted. Two hours had crept by and it was getting very late in the evening. Some of the party were, as Ann said, "yawning their heads off." Lluella and Heavy had camped down upon the old buffalo-robe before the fire and were already more than half asleep.

"I do wish they'd come back," muttered Bob Steele to Isadore Phelps. "We can't tell in here whether the storm has stopped, or not. I don't just fancy staying in this cave all night if there's any possible chance of getting to Mr. Tingley's house."

"Don't know what can be keeping those folks. I believe I could have crept on my hands and knees through the whole hill, and back again, before this time," returned Busy Izzy, in a very sleepy voice.

"Now, you can talk as you please," said Ann Hicks, with sudden decision, "but I'm going a short distance along that tunnel and see if the lantern is in sight."

"I'm with you!" exclaimed Bob.

"Me, too," joined in Helen, jumping up with alacrity.

"Now, some more of you will go off and get lost," cried Belle. "I—I wish we were all home. I'm—I'm sorry we came to this old island."

"Baby!" ejaculated her brother, poking her. "Do be still. Ralph isn't going to get lost—what d'ye think he is?"

"How'll we see our way?" Helen asked Bob and Ann.

"Feel it. We'll go in the dark. Then we can see their lantern the quicker."

"There's no wood here fit for torches," Bob admitted. "And I have plenty of matches. Come on! We sha'n't get lost."

"What do you really suppose has happened to them?" demanded Helen of Bob, as soon as they were out of hearing of the camp.

"Give it up. Something extraordinary—that's positive," declared the big fellow.

They crept through the tunnel, Bob lighting a match occasionally, until they reached the first crack in the roof, open to the sky. It was not snowing very hard.

"Of course they wouldn't have tried climbing up here to get out," queried Helen.

"Of course not!" exclaimed Ann. "What for?"

"No," said Bobbins. "They kept straight ahead—and so will we."

In five minutes, however, when they stopped, whispering, in a little chamber, Ann suddenly seized her companions and commanded them to hold their breath!

"I hear something," she whispered.

The others strained their ears to hear, too. In a moment a stone rattled. Then there sounded an unmistakable footstep upon the rock. Somebody was approaching.

"They're coming back?" asked Helen, doubtfully.

"Hush!" commanded Ann again. "Whoever it is, he has no light. It can't be Ruth."

Much heavier boots than those the girl of the Red Mill wore now rattled over the loose stones. Ann pulled the other two down beside her where she crouched in the corner.

"Wait!" she breathed.

"Can it be some wild animal?" asked Helen.

"With boots on? I bet!" scoffed Bob.

It was pitch dark. The three crouching together in the corner of the little chamber were not likely to attract the attention of this marauder, if all went well. But their hearts beat fast as the rustle of the approaching footsteps grew louder.

There loomed up a man's figure. It looked too big to be either Tom or Ralph, and it passed on with an assured step. He needed no lamp to find a path that seemed well known.

"Who—what—"

"Hush, Helen!" commanded Ann.

"But he's going right to the cave—and he carried a gun."

"I didn't see the gun," whispered Ann.

"I did," agreed Bob, squeezing Helen's arm. "It was a rifle. Do you suppose there is any danger?"

"It couldn't be anybody hunting us, do you suppose?" queried Helen, in a shaken voice. "Anybody from the house?"

"Preston!" exclaimed Ann.

"How would he know the way to get into this tunnel?" returned Bob. "Come on! let's spy on him. I'm worried now about Tom and the others."

"You don't suppose anything has happened to Ruthie?" whispered Helen. "Oh! you don't believe *that*, Bobbins?"

"Come on!" grunted the big fellow, and took the advance.

They were careful of their own footsteps over the loose stones. The person ahead acted as though he had an idea he was alone.

Nor did they overtake him until they had passed the open crack in the roof of the tunnel. Somebody laughed in the cavern ahead—then the girls all shouted.

The marauder stopped, uttering an astonished ejaculation. Bob and the two girls halted, too, but in a moment the person ahead turned, and came striding toward them, evidently fleeing from the sound of the voices.

Ann and Helen were really frightened, and with faint cries, shrank back. Bob *had* to be brave. He leaped forward to meet the person with the rifle, crying:

"Hold on, there!"

Alice B. Emerson

"Ha!" exclaimed the other and advanced the rifle until the muzzle touched Bob Steele's breast. The boy was naturally frightened—how could he help being? But he showed pluck. He did not move.

"What do you want in here? Who are you?" asked Bob, quietly.

"Goodness me!" gasped the other, and dropped the butt of his rifle to the ground. "You sure did startle me. You're one of those boys staying with the Tingleys?"

"Yes."

"And here's a couple of the girls. Not Ruth Fielding?"

"Oh, Jerry Sheming!" cried Ann, running forward. "You might have shot him with that gun."

"Not unless I'd loaded it first," replied Jerry, with a quiet chuckle. "But you folks scared me quite as much as I did you—Why, it's Miss Hicks and Miss Cameron."

"Where is Ruth?" demanded Ann, anxiously.

"And Tom?" joined in Helen.

"And how did you get back here to Cliff Island?" asked Bob. "We understood that you'd been railroaded out of the country."

"Hold on! hold on!" exclaimed Jerry. "Let's hear first about Miss Fielding. Where's she gone? How came you folks in this cave?"

Helen was the one who told him. She related all the

circumstances very briefly, but in a way to give Jerry a clear understanding of the situation.

"They've wandered off to the right. I know where they must be," said Jerry, decidedly. "I'll go find them. And then I'll get you all out of here. It has almost stopped snowing now."

"But how did you find your way back here to the island?" Bob demanded again.

"I ain't going to be beat by Blent," declared Jerry Sheming, doggedly. "I am going to have another look through the caves before I leave for good, and don't you forget it.

"The engine on that train yesterday morning broke a piston rod and had to stop down the lake shore. I hopped off and hid on the far bank, watching the island. If you folks hadn't come over this way to fish this morning, I'd been across before the storm began.

"I was pretty well turned around in the storm, and have been traveling a long time. But I got to the brook at last, and then worked my way up it and into the other end of this cave. I was going up there after my lantern—"

"Ruth and the others have it," explained Helen, quickly.

"Then I'll go find them at once. I know my way around pretty well in the dark. I couldn't get really lost in this cave," and Jerry laughed, shortly.

"I've got matches if you want them," said Bob.

"Got a plenty, thanks. You folks go back to your friends, and I'll hunt out Miss Fielding in a jiffy."

Alice B. Emerson

Jerry turned away at once, and soon passed out of their sight in the gloom. As Helen and the others hurried back to the anxious party at the campfire, Jerry went straightway to the most satisfactory discovery of all his life.

CHAPTER XXV

THE TREASURE BOX

When Jerry met Ruth and her companions coming slowly from the little cave, the boys bearing the heavy, ironbound box between them, he knew instantly what it was—his uncle's chest in which he had kept his money and papers.

"It's yours to hide again if you want to, Jerry," Ruth told him, when the excitement of the meeting had passed, and explanations were over. "It was what both you and Rufus Blent have been looking for, and I believe you have the best right to it"

"It belongs to Uncle Pete. And Uncle Pete shall have it," declared the backwoods boy. "Why, do you know, I believe if Uncle Pete once had this box in his possession again that he might recover his mind?"

"Oh, I hope so!" Ruth cried.

First, however, the crowd of young folk had to be led through the long tunnel and out into the open air. It was agreed that nothing was to be said to anybody but Mr. Tingley about the treasure box. And the boys and girls, too, agreed to say nothing at the house about Jerry's having

Alice B. Emerson

returned to his cave.

When they reached the brook, there were lights about the island, and guns being fired. The entire household of Tingley Lodge was out on the hunt for the lost ones.

The boys and girls were home and in bed in another hour, and Mrs. Tingley was vastly relieved.

"Never again will I take the responsibility of such a crowd!" declared the harassed lady. "My own children are enough; a dozen and a half active young ones like these would send me to the madhouse in another week!"

But the girls from Briarwood and their boy friends continued to have a delightful time during the remainder of their stay at Cliff Island, although their adventures were less strenuous than those that have been related. They went away, in the end, to take up their school duties, pronouncing their vacation on the island one of the most enjoyable they had ever experienced.

"Something to keep up our hearts for the rest of the school year," declared Heavy. "And you'll like us better, too, when we're gone, Mrs. Tingley. We *all*—even The Fox, here— have a good side to our characters."

Even Ann Hicks went back to Briarwood with pleasant expectations. She had learned to understand her mates better during this holiday, and all the girls at Briarwood were prepared to welcome the western girl now with more kindness than before.

We may believe that Ruth and her girl friends were all busy and happy during that next half-year at Briarwood, and we may meet them again in the midst of their work and fun in the next volume of the series, entitled "Ruth Fielding at Sunrise Farm; Or, What Became of the Raby Orphans."

Ruth Fielding, however, did not leave Cliff Island before being assured that the affairs of Jerry Sheming and his uncle would be set right. As it chanced, the very day the crowd had gone fishing Mr. Tingley had received a letter from the head doctor of the hospital, to whom the gentleman had written inquiring about old Peter Tilton.

The patient had improved immensely. That he was eccentric was true, but he had probably always been so, the doctor said. The old man was worrying over the loss of what he called his treasure box, and when Ruth confided to Mr. Tingley the truth about Jerry's return and the discovery of the ironbound box, Mr. Tingley determined to take matters into his own hands.

He first went to the cave and had a long talk with Jerry. Then he had his team of horses put to the sledge, and he and Jerry and the box drove the entire length of Lake Tallahaska, struck into a main road to the county asylum, and made an unexpected call upon the poor old hunter, who had been so long confined in that institution.

"It was jest what Uncle Pete needed to wake him up," Jerry declared to Ruth, when he saw her some weeks later. "He knowed the box and had always carried the key of it about his neck on a string. They didn't know what it was at the 'sylum, but they let him keep the key.

"And when he opened it, sure enough there was lots of papers and a couple of bags of money. I don't know how much, but Mr. Tingley got Uncle Pete to trust a bank with the money, and it'll be mine some day. Uncle Pete's going to pay my way through school with some of it, he says."

Alice B. Emerson

"But the title to the island?" demanded the excited girl of the Red Mill. "How did that come out? Did your uncle have any deed to it? What of that mean old Rufus Blent?"

"Jest you hold your hosses, Miss Ruth," laughed Jerry. "I'm comin' to that."

"But you are coming to it awfully slow, Jerry," complained the eager girl.

"No. I'll tell you quick's I can," he declared. "Uncle Pete had papers. He had been buying a part of the island from Blent on installments, and had paid the old rascal a good part of the price. But when Blent found out that uncle's papers were buried under the landslide he thought he could play a sharp trick and resell to Mr. Tingley. You see, the installment deeds were not recorded.

"However, Mr. Tingley's lawyers made old Blent get right down and howl for mercy—yes, they did! There was a strong case of conspiracy against him. That's still hanging fire.

"But Mr. Tingley says he will not push that, considering Rufus did all he was told to about the title money. He gave Uncle Pete back every cent he had paid in on the Cliff Island property, with interest compounded, and a good lump sum of money beside as a bonus.

"Then Uncle Pete made Mr. Tingley's title good, and we're going to live at the lodge during the closed season, as caretakers. That pleases Uncle Pete, for he couldn't be very well content anywhere else but on Cliff Island."

"Oh, Jerry! I am so glad it has come out all right for you," cried the girl of the Red Mill. "And so will all the other girls be when I tell them. And Uncle Jabez and Aunt Alvirah—for *they* are interested in your welfare, too."

"You're mighty kind, Miss Ruth," said the backwoods boy, bashfully. "I—I'm thinking I've got a lot more to thank *you* for than I ever can express right proper."

"Oh, no! no more to me than to other folks," cried Ruth Fielding, earnestly, for it had always been her natural instinct to help people, and she did not wish to be thanked for it.

That being the case, neither Jerry nor the writer must say anything more about the matter.

THE END

Alice B. Emerson

Choose from Thousands of 1stWorldLibrary Classics By

A. M. Barnard
Ada Leverson
Adolphus William Ward
Aesop
Agatha Christie
Alexander Aaronsohn
Alexander Kielland
Alexandre Dumas
Alfred Gatty
Alfred Ollivant
Alice Duer Miller
Alice Turner Curtis
Alice Dunbar
Allen Chapman
Alleyne Ireland
Ambrose Bierce
Amelia E. Barr
Amory H. Bradford
Andrew Lang
Andrew McFarland Davis
Andy Adams
Angela Brazil
Anna Alice Chapin
Anna Sewell
Annie Besant
Annie Hamilton Donnell
Annie Payson Call
Annie Roe Carr
Annonaymous
Anton Chekhov
Archibald Lee Fletcher
Arnold Bennett
Arthur C. Benson
Arthur Conan Doyle
Arthur M. Winfield
Arthur Ransome
Arthur Schnitzler
Arthur Train
Atticus
B.H. Baden-Powell
B. M. Bower
B. C. Chatterjee
Baroness Emmuska Orczy
Baroness Orczy
Basil King
Bayard Taylor
Ben Macomber
Bertha Muzzy Bower
Bjornstjerne Bjornson

Booth Tarkington
Boyd Cable
Bram Stoker
C. Collodi
C. E. Orr
C. M. Ingleby
Carolyn Wells
Catherine Parr Traill
Charles A. Eastman
Charles Amory Beach
Charles Dickens
Charles Dudley Warner
Charles Farrar Browne
Charles Ives
Charles Kingsley
Charles Klein
Charles Hanson Towne
Charles Lathrop Pack
Charles Romyn Dake
Charles Whibley
Charles Willing Beale
Charlotte M. Braeme
Charlotte M. Yonge
Charlotte Perkins Stetson
Clair W. Hayes
Clarence Day Jr.
Clarence E. Mulford
Clemence Housman
Confucius
Coningsby Dawson
Cornelis DeWitt Wilcox
Cyril Burleigh
D. H. Lawrence
Daniel Defoe
David Garnett
Dinah Craik
Don Carlos Janes
Donald Keyhoe
Dorothy Kilner
Dougan Clark
Douglas Fairbanks
E. Nesbit
E. P. Roe
E. Phillips Oppenheim
E. S. Brooks
Earl Barnes
Edgar Rice Burroughs
Edith Van Dyne
Edith Wharton

Edward Everett Hale
Edward J. O'Biren
Edward S. Ellis
Edwin L. Arnold
Eleanor Atkins
Eleanor Hallowell Abbott
Eliot Gregory
Elizabeth Gaskell
Elizabeth McCracken
Elizabeth Von Arnim
Ellem Key
Emerson Hough
Emilie F. Carlen
Emily Bronte
Emily Dickinson
Enid Bagnold
Enilor Macartney Lane
Erasmus W. Jones
Ernie Howard Pie
Ethel May Dell
Ethel Turner
Ethel Watts Mumford
Eugene Sue
Eugenie Foa
Eugene Wood
Eustace Hale Ball
Evelyn Everett-green
Everard Cotes
F. H. Cheley
F. J. Cross
F. Marion Crawford
Fannie E. Newberry
Federick Austin Ogg
Ferdinand Ossendowski
Fergus Hume
Florence A. Kilpatrick
Fremont B. Deering
Francis Bacon
Francis Darwin
Frances Hodgson Burnett
Frances Parkinson Keyes
Frank Gee Patchin
Frank Harris
Frank Jewett Mather
Frank L. Packard
Frank V. Webster
Frederic Stewart Isham
Frederick Trevor Hill
Frederick Winslow Taylor

Friedrich Kerst
Friedrich Nietzsche
Fyodor Dostoyevsky
G.A. Henty
G.K. Chesterton
Gabrielle E. Jackson
Garrett P. Serviss
Gaston Leroux
George A. Warren
George Ade
Geroge Bernard Shaw
George Cary Eggleston
George Durston
George Ebers
George Eliot
George Gissing
George MacDonald
George Meredith
George Orwell
George Sylvester Viereck
George Tucker
George W. Cable
George Wharton James
Gertrude Atherton
Gordon Casserly
Grace E. King
Grace Gallatin
Grace Greenwood
Grant Allen
Guillermo A. Sherwell
Gulielma Zollinger
Gustav Flaubert
H. A. Cody
H. B. Irving
H.C. Bailey
H. G. Wells
H. H. Munro
H. Irving Hancock
H. R. Naylor
H. Rider Haggard
H. W. C. Davis
Haldeman Julius
Hall Caine
Hamilton Wright Mabie
Hans Christian Andersen
Harold Avery
Harold McGrath
Harriet Beecher Stowe
Harry Castlemon
Harry Coghill
Harry Houidini

Hayden Carruth
Helent Hunt Jackson
Helen Nicolay
Hendrik Conscience
Hendy David Thoreau
Henri Barbusse
Henrik Ibsen
Henry Adams
Henry Ford
Henry Frost
Henry James
Henry Jones Ford
Henry Seton Merriman
Henry W Longfellow
Herbert A. Giles
Herbert Carter
Herbert N. Casson
Herman Hesse
Hildegard G. Frey
Homer
Honore De Balzac
Horace B. Day
Horace Walpole
Horatio Alger Jr.
Howard Pyle
Howard R. Garis
Hugh Lofting
Hugh Walpole
Humphry Ward
Ian Maclaren
Inez Haynes Gillmore
Irving Bacheller
Isabel Cecilia Williams
Isabel Hornibrook
Israel Abrahams
Ivan Turgenev
J.G.Austin
J. Henri Fabre
J. M. Barrie
J. M. Walsh
J. Macdonald Oxley
J. R. Miller
J. S. Fletcher
J. S. Knowles
J. Storer Clouston
J. W. Duffield
Jack London
Jacob Abbott
James Allen
James Andrews
James Baldwin

James Branch Cabell
James DeMille
James Joyce
James Lane Allen
James Lane Allen
James Oliver Curwood
James Oppenheim
James Otis
James R. Driscoll
Jane Abbott
Jane Austen
Jane L. Stewart
Janet Aldridge
Jens Peter Jacobsen
Jerome K. Jerome
Jessie Graham Flower
John Buchan
John Burroughs
John Cournos
John F. Kennedy
John Gay
John Glasworthy
John Habberton
John Joy Bell
John Kendrick Bangs
John Milton
John Philip Sousa
John Taintor Foote
Jonas Lauritz Idemil Lie
Jonathan Swift
Joseph A. Altsheler
Joseph Carey
Joseph Conrad
Joseph E. Badger Jr
Joseph Hergesheimer
Joseph Jacobs
Jules Vernes
Julian Hawthrone
Julie A Lippmann
Justin Huntly McCarthy
Kakuzo Okakura
Karle Wilson Baker
Kate Chopin
Kenneth Grahame
Kenneth McGaffey
Kate Langley Bosher
Kate Langley Bosher
Katherine Cecil Thurston
Katherine Stokes
L. A. Abbot
L. T. Meade

L. Frank Baum
Latta Griswold
Laura Dent Crane
Laura Lee Hope
Laurence Housman
Lawrence Beasley
Leo Tolstoy
Leonid Andreyev
Lewis Carroll
Lewis Sperry Chafer
Lilian Bell
Lloyd Osbourne
Louis Hughes
Louis Joseph Vance
Louis Tracy
Louisa May Alcott
Lucy Fitch Perkins
Lucy Maud Montgomery
Luther Benson
Lydia Miller Middleton
Lyndon Orr
M. Corvus
M. H. Adams
Margaret E. Sangster
Margret Howth
Margaret Vandercook
Margaret W. Hungerford
Margret Penrose
Maria Edgeworth
Maria Thompson Daviess
Mariano Azuela
Marion Polk Angellotti
Mark Overton
Mark Twain
Mary Austin
Mary Catherine Crowley
Mary Cole
Mary Hastings Bradley
Mary Roberts Rinehart
Mary Rowlandson
M. Wollstonecraft Shelley
Maud Lindsay
Max Beerbohm
Myra Kelly
Nathaniel Hawthrone
Nicolo Machiavelli
O. F. Walton
Oscar Wilde

Owen Johnson
P.G. Wodehouse
Paul and Mabel Thorne
Paul G. Tomlinson
Paul Severing
Percy Brebner
Percy Keese Fitzhugh
Peter B. Kyne
Plato
Quincy Allen
R. Derby Holmes
R. L. Stevenson
R. S. Ball
Rabindranath Tagore
Rahul Alvares
Ralph Bonehill
Ralph Henry Barbour
Ralph Victor
Ralph Waldo Emmerson
Rene Descartes
Ray Cummings
Rex Beach
Rex E. Beach
Richard Harding Davis
Richard Jefferies
Richard Le Gallienne
Robert Barr
Robert Frost
Robert Gordon Anderson
Robert L. Drake
Robert Lansing
Robert Lynd
Robert Michael Ballantyne
Robert W. Chambers
Rosa Nouchette Carey
Rudyard Kipling
Saint Augustine
Samuel B. Allison
Samuel Hopkins Adams
Sarah Bernhardt
Sarah C. Hallowell
Selma Lagerlof
Sherwood Anderson
Sigmund Freud
Standish O'Grady
Stanley Weyman
Stella Benson
Stella M. Francis

Stephen Crane
Stewart Edward White
Stijn Streuvels
Swami Abhedananda
Swami Parmananda
T. S. Ackland
T. S. Arthur
The Princess Der Ling
Thomas A. Janvier
Thomas A Kempis
Thomas Anderton
Thomas Bailey Aldrich
Thomas Bulfinch
Thomas De Quincey
Thomas Dixon
Thomas H. Huxley
Thomas Hardy
Thomas More
Thornton W. Burgess
U. S. Grant
Upton Sinclair
Valentine Williams
Various Authors
Vaughan Kester
Victor Appleton
Victor G. Durham
Victoria Cross
Virginia Woolf
Wadsworth Camp
Walter Camp
Walter Scott
Washington Irving
Wilbur Lawton
Wilkie Collins
Willa Cather
Willard F. Baker
William Dean Howells
William le Queux
W. Makepeace Thackeray
William W. Walter
William Shakespeare
Winston Churchill
Yei Theodora Ozaki
Yogi Ramacharaka
Young E. Allison
Zane Grey

www.ingramcontent.com/pod-product-compliance
Lightning Source LLC
Chambersburg PA
CBHW031346170626
46807CB00002B/853